Tipbook
Music for Kids and Teens

A Guide for Parents and Caregivers

Hugo Pinksterboer

Tipbook
Music for Kids and Teens

A Guide for Parents and Caregivers

HAL•LEONARD®

The Complete Guide to Your Instrument!

Copyright © 2006, 2010 by The Tipbook Company bv

All rights reserved. No part of this book may be reproduced in any form, without written permission, except by a newspaper or magazine reviewer who wishes to quote brief passages in connection with a review.

The publisher and author have done their best to ensure the accuracy and timeliness of all the information in this Tipbook; however, they can accept no responsibility for any loss, injury, or inconvenience sustained as a result of information or advice contained in this book. Trademarks, user names, and certain illustrations have been used in this book solely to identify the products or instruments discussed. Such use does not imply endorsement by or affiliation with the trademark owner(s).

First edition published in 2004 by
The Tipbook Company bv, The Netherlands

Second edition published in 2010 by
Hal Leonard Books

An Imprint of Hal Leonard Corporation
7777 West Bluemound Road
Milwaukee, WI 53213

Trade Book Division Editorial Offices
33Plymouth Street, Montclair, NJ 07042

Printed in the United States of America

Book design by Gijs Bierenbroodspot

Library of Congress Cataloging-in-Publication Data

Pinksterboer, Hugo.
 Tipbook music for kids and teens : a guide for parents and caregivers / Hugo Pinksterboer. -- 2nd ed.
   p. cm.
 Originally published: Netherlands : Tipbook Co., 2004.
 Includes index.
 ISBN 978-1-4234-6526-3 (pbk.)
 1. Music--Instruction and study--Parent participation. I. Title. II. Title: Music for kids and teens.
 MT1.P557 2010
 372.87--dc22

2010046519

www.halleonard.com

Thanks!

For their information, inspiration, expertise, time, and help, we'd like to thank the following musicians, educators, parents, and other national and international experts: Maribeth Barrons, Steve Clover, Sherise Parker-Alofs, Davina Cowan, Bob Wendel (Robert Wendel Music, NY), Graham Lyons, Guntram Wolf (instrument maker, Germany), Hugo Rodriguez (Antigua Winds), Eugene Monnig (Cadenza Music, Minnesota), Ron Payne (Music Teacher Magazine), Jojo Mayer, Henk Rensink, Bert Steinman, Albert van Ee, Mia Dreese (NFG, Dutch Flute Association), Lies Vledder (European String Teachers Association), Ad van Dun, Maarten Visser (Flutelab), Ruud van der Meulen (Probasse), Jan van den Eijnden (Unisono), and the dozens of experts who contributed to the educational issues in the first fourteen Tipbooks.

About the Author

Journalist, writer, and musician Hugo Pinksterboer, author of The Tipbook Series, has published hundreds of interviews, articles, and reviews for national and international music magazines, and contributed to music method books, courses for music sales people, and a wide variety of other publications.

About the Designer

Illustrator, designer, and musician Gijs Bierenbroodspot has worked as an art director for a wide variety of magazines and has developed numerous ad campaigns. While searching in vain for information about saxophone mouthpieces, he got the idea for this series of books on music and musical instruments. He is responsible for the layout and illustrations for all of the Tipbooks.

Acknowledgments

Cover photo: René Vervloet
Editors: Michael J. Collins and Rachel Stevens

Anything missing?

Any omissions? Any areas that could be improved? Please go to www.tipbook.com to contact us, or send an email to info@tipbook.com. Thanks!

Contents

X Introduction

XII See and Hear What You Read with Tipcodes
The Tipcodes in this book give you access to short videos, sound files, and other additional information at www.tipbook.com.

1 Chapter 1. Music Essentials
Music is believed to make you smarter; it is both fun and relaxing; it can help you make friends, and it enhances both your social skills and your self-esteem. Plenty of reasons to take your child's musical education seriously!

9 Chapter 2. Phases and Learning Styles
A quick look at the main phases of musical development, and children's learning styles.

21 Chapter 3. Learning to Play
All aspects of learning to play an instrument or sing: from music programs for infants to professional education, group teaching versus private teaching, where to find a good teacher and how to recognize one, costs, and much more.

73 Chapter 4. Practicing
Learning to play an instrument requires practice — but practice isn't always fun. Helpful hints on how to make practicing effective and entertaining, practice facilities and tools, hearing protection, sound insulation, and more.

111	**Chapter 5. Guidance and Motivation**
	Tips on how to keep children playing music.
119	**Chapter 6. Borrowing, Renting, or Buying?**
	Essential information on how and where to get an instrument for your child and on the additional costs of playing an instrument.
141	**Chapter 7. Which Instrument?**
	Choosing the right instrument is essential for long-lasting musical fun.
165	**Chapter 8. Playing Together**
	The importance of making music in a group, and a quick guide to the main types of bands, orchestras, and other groups.
183	**Chapter 9. The Instruments**
	An introduction to the most popular and some lesser-known instruments.
209	**Chapter 10. Being Prepared**
	How to deal with audition anxiety, exam nerves, and stage fright.
219	**Glossary**
222	**Tipcode List**
	All Music for Kids and Teens Tipcodes listed.
223	**Want to Know More?**
	Information about relevant books, magazines, websites, and other resources.
230	**Essential Data**
	Four pages for listing important phone numbers, websites, instrument data, and other relevant information.

CONTENTS

234 *Index*

239 *The Tipbook Series*

Introduction

Playing a musical instrument is a fun, inspiring, and rewarding pastime. It can be a demanding pastime as well, for both children and you, their parents or caregivers. It's also a hobby that requires many small and large decisions: which instrument to play, buying or renting an instrument (and should it be new, or pre-owned?), which teacher to go to, whether to take exams or go to competitions, when to practice, how to develop a good practice routine, and how not to bother neighbors and housemates.

While the answers to many of these questions may come naturally, it is good to have easy access to well-founded, unbiased, and accessible background information on these and all related subjects. *Tipbook Music for Kids and Teens* offers just that.

The same idea
Rather than presenting one professional's opinion on the subject, *Tipbook Music for Kids and Teens* provides you with the insights, ideas, and experiences of various music teachers and other experts. Their thoughts may sometimes strongly differ — but in the end, they all promote the same idea: Let your children play music!

Your decision
The information in this book is intended to help you make the right decisions when it comes to the musical education of your

INTRODUCTION

children. It doesn't tell you what to decide, however, if only because each child is different, and your ideas of education in general may not be the same as those of your friends or neighbors. So for example, this book lists both the pros and the cons of taking music exams, it shares a variety of ideas on purchasing instruments and many other subjects, and it looks at the best way to teach children from various perspectives, taking their learning styles into account.

Guidance and motivation
Likewise, this book holds a lot of information on how to inspire kids to keep on practicing, and it offers a large number of tips on guidance and motivation. No doubt, some of them will inspire you to come up with even more ideas.

Instruments
Two chapters are dedicated to musical instruments, one focusing on choosing the right instrument, the other on basic instrument knowledge. If you want to know more about a certain instrument, please check pages 239–243 to see if there is a Tipbook available on the subject, or visit www.tipbook.com to find the latest additions to the series.

Glossary and index
Like all other Tipbooks, this book offers you a glossary and an index, allowing you to quickly look up most relevant terms and to find what you're looking for, making the information as accessible as possible. Enjoy!

— Hugo Pinksterboer

See and Hear What You Read with Tipcodes

www.tipbook.com

In addition to the illustrations on the following pages, Tipbooks offer you a new way to see — and even hear — what you are reading about. The Tipcodes that you will come across throughout this book give you access to short videos, sound files, and other additional information at www.tipbook.com.

Here's how it works: page 187 of this book shows a nylon-string and a steel-string guitar. The section below this illustration is marked **Tipcode KIDS-009**. Type in that code on the Tipcode page at www.tipbook.com, and you will see and hear a brief demonstration of the different timbres of the instruments that are covered on these pages. Similar video examples are available on a variety of subjects; other Tipcodes will link to a sound file.

Tipcode KIDS-009
To hear the difference between a nylon-string and a steel-string acoustic guitar, play this Tipcode.

SEE AND HEAR WHAT YOU READ WITH TIPCODES

Repeat
If you miss something the first time, you can of course replay the Tipcode. And if it all happens too fast, use the pause button below the movie window.

Tipcodes listed
For your convenience, the Tipcodes presented in this book are listed on page 222. The Tipcodes in this book mainly include demonstrations of a wide range of musical instruments, ranging from the clarinet voices to violin and viola, nylon-string and steel-string guitars, flutes, and drums.

Plug-ins
If the software you need to view the videos is not yet installed on your computer, you'll automatically be told which software you

First, make your selection: Tipcode, chords and fingering charts, or the glossary.

The Tipcode window displays movies, photo series, fingering charts, chords, and explanations of the words used in this book.

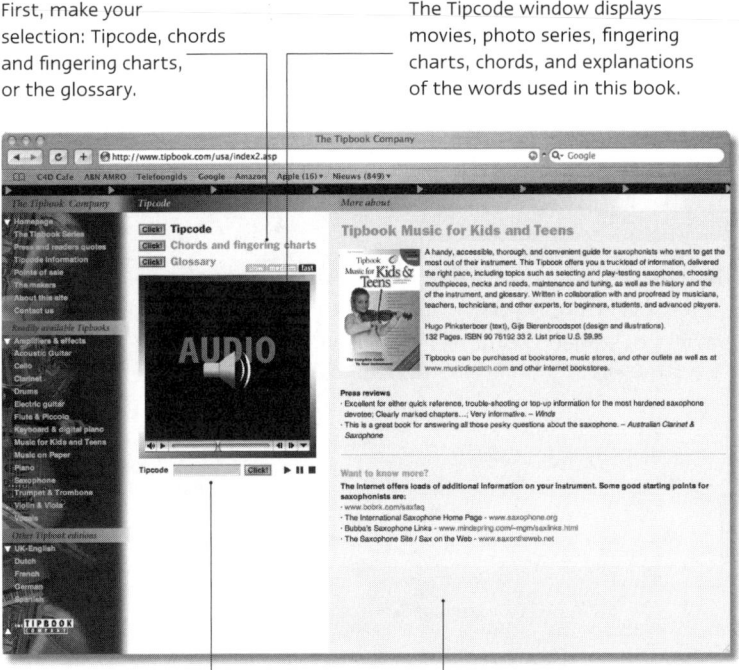

Enter a Tipcode here and click on the button. Want to see it again? Click again.

These links take you directly to other interesting sites.

need, and where you can download it. This type of software is free. Questions? Check out 'About this site' at www.tipbook.com.

Still more at www.tipbook.com
You can find even more information at www.tipbook.com. For instance, you can look up words in the glossaries of all the Tipbooks published to date. There are chord diagrams for guitarists and pianists; fingering charts for saxophonists, clarinetists, and flutists; and rudiments for drummers. Also included are links to most of the websites mentioned in the Want to Know More? section of each Tipbook.

Tipbook
Music for Kids and Teens

A Guide for Parents and Caregivers

1

Music Essentials

Playing music, on any instrument and in any style, is a very rewarding pastime for anyone, at any age — and especially for children. It enhances their creativity, teaches them problem solving, and trains their memory; it helps make them smarter and improves their social skills. In short, children who learn to perform music are likely to perform better in many aspects of life. That makes music more than just a way to pass time: It is considered an essential element of your child's education.

CHAPTER 1

Providing children with a musical education truly helps to educate them in every sense of the word. As a parent, you have a crucial role in the musical success of your children, whether they want to play an instrument or sing just for fun, or become a professional musician — or both.

Their choice...
Many children are naturally and deeply drawn to playing music. If your kids are, you'll have a hard time stopping them. They know what they want to play and they will beg for an instrument and music lessons, because they think it will be fun, or because their friends do it and they want to be part of the action, or for any other reason. Other children, however, may not think even think about playing music until you, the school's music teacher, or someone else suggests it to them. At that point, they may be just as enthusiastic and self-motivated, but chances are they'll need more support and guidance.

... or yours
Some parents choose to guide their children more actively, getting them piano lessons at age six, or violin lessons at age four, for example. No questions asked, no explanations given. Music lessons are simply presented as an inherent part of the child's education, much like going to school.

Not a fad
No matter how children start their musical 'careers,' your guidance and support is essential. If you think music is a vital aspect of their education — as many professionals do — you may take your children to special music programs long before they can talk, or even walk. Alternatively, you can choose to just wait and see what happens, and be there when your child is ready.

Playing music is fun
If you feel that your child's desire to play music is nothing more than a fad, you risk influencing your child to think likewise. As a result, you will be proven right, but no one has gained. Another extreme would be to force your children to play no matter what. Children should primarily associate playing music with fun,

MUSIC ESSENTIALS

rather than with the many duties they otherwise have to face — which doesn't mean you should allow them to neglect practice just because they don't feel like it. If they have expressed the desire to play, keep them to their part of the deal: They wanted to play the instrument that you purchased for them, and they can't just let go without even trying.

Play or sing
One of the best ways to get your children interested in playing music is to play yourself. Just like your children learn to walk and talk by watching you and listening to you, they will develop an interest in music if they see and hear you play from time to time. And if you don't play? Sing to them. You can rest assured that your vocal abilities are absolutely irrelevant. It is your enthusiasm that will inspire them, not the quality of your performance.

At any level
Every child can learn to play music or sing, just like people can learn to talk or drive a car. Playing computer games — which almost all children do — is often more complex than playing or 'operating' a musical instrument. And, when it comes to music, one of the many benefits is that you can enjoy playing at any level. You don't need to be really good in order to play and have fun, whether by yourself or in a musical group of some kind.

Fun
So first of all, making music is about having fun, whether it's playing by yourself, rehearsing with the school orchestra, performing with a marching band, setting up your own rock band, or working out a flute duet with the kid next door.

Smarter
Music is said to make children smarter, too. Research suggests that listening to a Mozart Sonata can improve one's spatial-temporal reasoning, be it for only ten minutes or so*. This type of reasoning, essential for success in math, science, chess, and checkers (and so on) seems to be enhanced long-term by learning to play an

* The so-called (and much debated) Mozart effect.

CHAPTER 1

instrument. Part of the explanation is that all these activities involve the recognition of certain patterns, and instrumental music instruction stimulates the same area of the brain that processes numbers and equations.

One of the relationships between music and math: Reading music requires an understanding (and may offer a clarification) of fractions. The shape of a note indicates the note's duration; there are whole notes, half notes, quarter notes, eighth notes, etc.

And more
But it doesn't stop there. Students who play a musical instrument score forty to fifty points higher on the verbal and mathematic sections of the SAT, for example, and evidence suggests that memory is improved. (Note that acting and dancing lessons can generate similar results!)

And yet more
If you play music, you'll have to find ways to tackle all kinds of problems: How to deal with this tricky bit, which fingering works best for this phrase, how to master this new piece, or how to memorize this section, etc. This helps improving general problem solving skills and analytical skills. Playing music can also foster writing skills, while learning to *read* music may help children to get better at speed-reading text, and increase their attention span. On a physical level, playing an instrument helps children develop fine motor skills, and eye-hand coordination will be improved.

Early start
An early start is often suggested to make things even more effective. Many experts state that it's best if children have their first active music experiences before the age of six or seven. Just listening to music, which can definitely help to raise your child's interest in learning to play an instrument, is not enough. Children have to really 'do music'. They need musical interaction in order to fully experience the benefits of this form of art. Many expectant parents follow prenatal programs based on the theory that children who are exposed to music while still in the womb tend to be more relaxed, sleep better, are easier to nurse, and develop at a faster rate.

In any case, it won't hurt — and if playing music to your unborn child makes you feel good, it'll probably help your baby feel good too.

Social skills
Playing music in a band or an orchestra brings people together, and it helps children connect with others. Bands, orchestras, and choirs are a rich source of new friends, and offer a solid support system for your child as well. As a matter of fact, for many children, the social aspect is the main reason to play an instrument and be in a band at all.

Solo
So what about children who prefer to be by themselves? No problem. First, various instruments are very well suited for playing just by yourself, such as the guitar or the piano. Second, play-along CDs and similar media offer ample opportunity to play any instrument in the context of a 'virtual' band or ensemble — and you can only hope this makes your child want to join a real live band later on. This is more fun in the end, and playing in an ensemble can truly help children to deal with their inhibitions.

Teamwork
Teamwork is an essential element in making any type of ensemble succeed. Being in a band or orchestra teaches children how to work on a common task, and it helps them define their role and present their own voice in a smaller or larger group setting. It also teaches them to listen to others, and to tune in to their fellow musicians, in the broadest sense of the word. And if parents or siblings play an instrument or sing as well, making music at home can definitely help bring the family together.

Communication
Music is often described as a universal language (though some say it's neither universal nor a language). It helps bridge gaps between people of different abilities, cultures, ages, and political convictions. Also, learning to play an instrument allows children a fascinating way to communicate. After all, a musical performance can make people feel good, and it can make them dance, think, or relax.

CHAPTER 1

All alone
At the same time, learning to play an instrument is something you do all alone. Positively speaking, this teaches children self-discipline and time management skills. For example, it encourages them to find ways to use their practice time as effectively as possible. Most children need initial or continued guidance on both points, however. While kids usually don't need to be inspired to watch TV or play games, you will probably have to 'inspire' them to practice, from time to time, and help them use their time wisely. Specific tips follow in later chapters.

A stronger self
Playing music helps many children connect with themselves, gain confidence and self-esteem, and overcome shyness. Children who do not dare to speak up may learn how to do so through their instrument, and many have experienced that presenting a paper in class becomes much easier once they've learned to perform music onstage or play scales in front of fellow classmates. Conversely, there are children who need yoga classes or a drama program to help them overcome their musical stage fright. Things often work both ways.

Creativity
It goes without saying that playing music enhances creativity and provides a great means for self-expression. It also teaches active, rather than passive, listening. Most musicians, at any level, also develop a higher appreciation of other forms of art. And while music in itself is usually not considered a tool, such as reading, writing, and math, it most definitely helps you to use those tools creatively — at any age!

Relax
Making music helps reduce stress, as do most means of self-expression. Simply listening to music does so too, of course, but playing requires more focus, which definitely can help you forget your worries, at least for the time being. Likewise, playing music is a great means of emotional release. You can obviously let off steam by hitting a set of drums, but also by playing the flute, the piano, or any other instrument.

MUSIC ESSENTIALS

Health

Making music is even said to be good for your immune system, increasing the number of disease-fighting cells. These and other benefits of learning to play an instrument can last a lifetime. Senior citizens who play music tend not only to be healthier, but they are bothered less by anxiety, depression, and loneliness.

> **Less problems**
> Kids involved in music programs are less likely to develop disciplinary problems or drop out of school. Likewise, they tend to be less inclined to turn to drugs, commit crimes, or show antisocial behavior.

Everyone

One of the beauties of music is that virtually anyone can play, including children who are physically or mentally challenged, or other disabilities (musical instruments can be adapted to accommodate a number of physical impediments). For example, autistic children can use music to communicate. And above all, what counts is not how well you play, but simply that you play.

Paint, dance, play ball

So should every child play music? It would be fun, probably, but only if they really loved to do so. The truth is, however, that some children just don't like playing an instrument or singing, regardless of how happy and smart and healthy and cooperative and desirable they would get. You may want to encourage them to have a go at it anyway, which might be successful. But if they'd rather paint, dance, or play ball, it may be better to let them do just that. After all, many of the benefits of a musical education listed in this chapter also apply to a wide variety of other creative activities and sports.

Your costs

If your children *do* want to play music, be prepared to invest in their musical career, in various ways. One way, of course, is financially, as you'll have to pay for lessons, instruments,

CHAPTER 1

accessories, and so on. Also, you'll have to help your children set up and maintain a practice routine, keep them motivated when progress is slow or seemingly non-existent, or when other activities seem to grow more attractive. You may have to get them to and from their lessons and performances. And you may have to endure the often discordant sounds of practice: beginning violinists, budding drummers, or trumpeters playing scales are not always fun to listen to, after all. But it's definitely worth it. Have you ever met someone who regretted being able to play an instrument or sing?

2

Phases and Learning Styles

When growing up, children go through various phases of musical development. This chapter takes a closer look at those phases, and sheds some light on different learning styles. This information can be very helpful in guiding your child's musical education.

CHAPTER 2

Some children have an inherent talent for music. But is there such a thing as a 'non-musical' child? No, there isn't. Any child can learn to sing or play an instrument. Most so-called 'non-musical' children are simply those who've had no musical education, or who (sadly) simply believe themselves to be non-musical. Unfortunately, children who are told they are non-musical from an early age — usually by caregivers impatient with the time it took these kids to learn how to sing in tune or to move to the rhythm of a song — are likely to believe such messages, and they will purposefully shy away from attempting to learn or explore music.

Too soon?
Basically, you can't expose your child to music too soon. Special music education programs are available for children at any age, from newborns to toddlers and beyond. Quite a number of children start playing a 'real' instrument (mostly violin or piano) as soon as they're five or six years of age, or even younger.

Just listen
Any adult learning a new language knows that it takes a great deal of time and effort to do so. But young children are capable of learning a second language without any noticeable difficulty, just by listening to people who speak it — so it would seem only logical that they would pick up music just as easily.

Too late?
It is never too late for your child (or yourself!) to learn to play an instrument. Even children who start at fifteen or sixteen are usually able to join the school band after four or five months of lessons and some serious practicing. Quite a number of young drummers, bass players, and guitarists join garage bands the same week they first pick up an instrument. Actually, there are numerous professional musicians who started only in their teens; classical musicians, too, though they usually have their first lessons at a much younger age. More boys than girls first pick up an instrument in their mid to late teens. This is most likely due to the fact that there tend to be more boys than girls in the pop and rock bands that often inspire teenagers to start playing.

PHASES AND LEARNING STYLES

Don't make them wait
An essential tip: When children show an interest in playing an instrument, don't make them wait until the school's music program starts. Instead, find a private teacher and let them have a go at the instrument of their choice…

Too soon
… unless they're not yet physically ready to play that instrument, of course. In that case, try to come up with an alternative instrument that can satisfy their desire to play. Chapter 7 tells you all about choosing an instrument.

Pre-birth
Evidence suggests that even unborn children respond to music. Do they actually recognize music from the time before they were born? Some specialists say they do, but there's still a lot of debate, and such theories are of course difficult to prove. It is clear, however, that fetuses can hear sounds from some sixteen to twenty weeks after conception, and they appear to actually respond to music after about twenty-six weeks. Their perception is limited to lower frequencies, however, as high frequencies and complex sounds are muffled by the fluid in the womb. A tip: If you're pregnant, there is no need to put speakers on your belly. The womb is a quiet place, and sounds will surely travel there. As mentioned in Chapter 1, there are special prenatal programs that claim to stimulate the development of the fetus through sound.

Newborns
Newborn children can soon indicate what music they like. Between three and six months of age, they will actively respond to music and sounds in general. In a next phase, you will see that they become aware of where sounds are coming from. Around their first birthday they may already recognize songs they've heard before, and even 'sing' along.

First words
Most babies say their first words between eight and eighteen months. Singing songs to your baby is very likely to boost their language development.

CHAPTER 2

Toy instruments
Between ages one and two, most children become aware of the various types of music, and they will start articulating their responses to different songs. Also, they start moving to the music in a more coordinated way, and they will produce sounds by hitting things. You can guide this tendency in a musical direction by giving them any of the many children's age-appropriate toy instruments, such as drums, shakers, or xylophones, or even a toy piano.

An outline
Around their second birthday, many children start reproducing parts of songs they've heard, though you will be likely to hear more of a general outline than the exact notes and lyrics. Also, they tend to sing along at this age rather than sing by themselves. This implies that you can play an important role by singing with them. Around the age of three, when they begin to learn the lyrics to simple songs, they're likely to start singing by themselves. They may also make up their own songs. Also by this age, they will usually be able to distinguish differences in volume (dynamics), pitch (high and low notes), and tempo. Music appreciation classes can help speed up this process, making children more aware of these concepts.

Real lessons
As children grow older, they will develop an awareness of pitch and rhythm, and they learn to distinguish the sounds of different instruments. The scope of the songs they can sing increases as their vocabulary expands and as they gain more control over their vocal instrument. Likewise, their motor skills, coordination, and ability to focus will increase to a point where they get ready for their first 'real' music lessons — 'real' meaning they learn to really

When?
Some say that children can be ready for real lessons as soon as they're three years of age, but it may be better to wait until they're five, six, or seven, depending both on their personal development and on their instrument of choice (see pages 152–160).

play a bona fide instrument, rather than playing around with toy instruments.

The alphabet
There are various questionnaires available to assist in determining if a child is ready to start lessons. Some teachers suggest a child should be able to count to twenty-five or thirty, or to recite the alphabet to the letter H (or K, or Q…), and some specify exact minimum sizes of hands, arms, or other physical attributes that would indicate whether a child is ready. Instructors who depend on these 'qualifiers' may help raise the average level of their students' success, but they may also steer children, talented or not, away from their musical dreams. The love for music cannot be measured in physical dimensions or academic performance.

Practicing
For children to get the most out of their lessons, they must develop good practice habits. Under the age of seven or eight, however, children can hardly be expected to develop and maintain such a routine. Lessons for the very young are mostly about having fun and developing a love for music, rather than about steady progress and musical excellence.

Your input
Committing your child to serious music study at a very young age requires that you are actively involved. You will usually need to be present when they practice, for example, and various early childhood music programs not only require you to attend lessons, but to also continue lessons at home as your child's 'home teacher.' There's more on this on page 29.

Reading music
Children can learn to read music around the same time they're ready to learn to read text. There are all kinds of interactive games that can help your child read music in an easy, playful way.

Singing in tune
Most children are able to sing in tune around the age six or seven. By that time, most of them can also keep a basic beat, clapping

CHAPTER 2

their hands or dancing in time with the music. At that point, they have achieved basic musical competence. With a natural talent and enough support, some children can accomplish this much earlier. Six or seven-year-olds may also be able to figure out how to play a familiar melody on a piano or other keyboard instrument. Playing around with these and other instruments can even inspire their first compositions.

Fractional instruments

The choice of instruments for children under the age of six or seven is usually limited to the violin and other orchestral strings (which are available in smaller sizes; see page 126), piano or keyboard, perhaps guitar, and percussion. When they turn six or seven, they can choose from a larger (and growing!) number of downsized instruments. Examples are on pages 152-160.

The violin is one of the instruments that can be played by very young children.

All instruments

As children get a little older, having had the opportunity to listen to various styles of music, they will become more adept at actively distinguishing the sounds and characters of the wide variety of instruments available. This will help them to decide on an instrument. Most ten to twelve-year-olds can physically handle most 'adult-sized' instruments.

Teeth

Playing a wind instrument may exert additional pressure on the teeth. That's why some say that children who either wear braces or do not have their adult teeth yet should not play such an instrument — even though numerous kids have proven that it can be done. There's more on this sensitive subject on pages 59–64.

Early teens

The early teens are a time of many changes. Children who started playing at an earlier age may become more serious about their musical activities during these years — whether as a means of self-expression and self-exploration, to have fun, to make friends, to gain respect and increase self-esteem, or for any other reason. Some teens express an interest in playing an instrument for the first time in their lives. They may pick up a bass guitar to join friends in a garage band right away, or devote themselves to a lot of serious practice on the double bass (upright bass) so they can join the school orchestra — or anything in between.

Dropping out

Unfortunately, many children quit their musical activities in their early teens, for a wide variety of reasons. As children begin to discover and develop their personal and musical identities at this age, they may find out that they actually dislike the music or the instrument they initially chose — or they just want to do things differently than you or their teachers suggest. (Remember?)

Changes

The step from elementary school to junior high or middle school brings along a lot of other changes: new friends, single-subject teachers, academic pressure and related responsibilities, and so on. Likewise, all kinds of physical changes present themselves, from pimples to the mutation of boy's voices (with due effects on their singing, too). It is also the time that many kids get braces, which can hinder trumpeters, clarinetists and other wind instrument players (see pages 61–64). Finally, music teachers may and typically will be more demanding toward students of this age, which can spoil your child's pleasure in taking lessons. The sum total of these changes can easily be enough to make children want to stop playing the instrument they previously enjoyed so much.

Simple?

Nevertheless, proper guidance and sufficient patience may be all

CHAPTER 2

you need to encourage your children to continue their musical studies. This may be as simple as allowing them to switch from the saxophone to the clarinet (or vice versa), or to support their use of a computer as a musical tool in lieu of a traditional musical instrument. And hard as it may be, you might just have to accept their present lack of interest in music, and hope that they'll return to their instrument, or a different one, in the future. This may not happen until they leave the house, but even so, you can be happy that their early musical education paid off in the long run.

... from the saxophone to the clarinet...

TIPBOOK MUSIC FOR KIDS AND TEENS

PHASES AND LEARNING STYLES

LEARNING STYLES

People pick up and process information in different ways. While observing children as they grow up, you'll notice their different learning styles and modes of development. Guiding your child's musical education may become easier if you know a little about these styles.

Touch and eat
Babies explore things by touching them (tactile learning) and by putting them in their mouths (gustatory learning). These evolve into a mixture of three main learning styles: visual, auditory and physical.

- **Visual**: learning by reading, via images, or through other visuals. Visual learners prefer a map to a verbal explanation.

- **Auditory**: learning by listening. Auditory learners prefer a lecture to reading a textbook.

- **Physical**: learning by physically doing things. True physical learners can hardly sit still for more than five minutes and cannot talk without using their hands.

> ### All three
> Learning to play an instrument often requires elements from all three learning styles. You learn physically by actually 'operating' the instrument. Your auditory skills are required to hear yourself and your fellow musicians play, to understand your teacher, and to learn from hearing other musicians perform. The visual element comes into play when you're learning to read music, or chord diagrams or tabs (see pages 58–59).

TIP

Visual learners
Typical visual learners may get lost if you take away their sheet music or lyric sheet: Visual input is crucial to them. At the same

CHAPTER 2

time, they may easily pick up all kinds of playing tips and techniques from watching educational music DVDs or YouTube clips, for example. They're not very likely to become star improvisers. Visual learners may prefer instruments on which they can watch what they're doing — the positions of the fingers on a guitar neck or a keyboard, for example. They're less likely to choose a brass instrument, for example, because these instruments don't provide any type of visual feedback. In today's society, visual learning is the prevailing learning style: Most information is offered either in print, on TV, or online.

The left hand on the guitar...

Auditory learners

Children who easily memorize the lyrics of the songs you sing to them are probably auditory learners. They often possess a particularly strong musical instinct. Children who are able to play or sing a song they've heard just once, may be less motivated to learn how to read music — but there are many great (mainly non-classical) musicians and enthusiastic amateurs who never learned to read.

Physical learners

True physical learners tend to become drummers rather than flutists, or lead singers rather than choir boys or girls. They're usually more at home in a marching band than in a string quartet. They like action, and instead of waiting for an explanation or watching an educational DVD, they'd rather pick up the instrument and give it a go. They're probably the ones who like to maintain, adjust, and fix (or ruin, at first) their own instruments too. Physical learners are also known as bodily-kinesthetic or tactual-kinesthetic (T-K, K-T) learners.

PHASES AND LEARNING STYLES

One missing
Most people show a combination of the above learning styles, but one usually prevails. And even though visually and aurally challenged people are one learning mode short, there are many wonderful blind and even deaf professional musicians, as well as numerous sensory-impaired amateurs who love playing music.

More learning styles
There are many more ways to distinguish one learner from another. Some examples:

- **Physical learners** are often active learners. They prefer to try things out rather than think of a plan beforehand, which is what a reflective learner would do.

- **Social (interpersonal) learners** tend to enjoy their group lessons and playing in a band more than their solitary practicing sessions, while solitary (intrapersonal) learners will often choose an instrument that allows them to play all by themselves, such as a home keyboard, the piano, or the guitar.

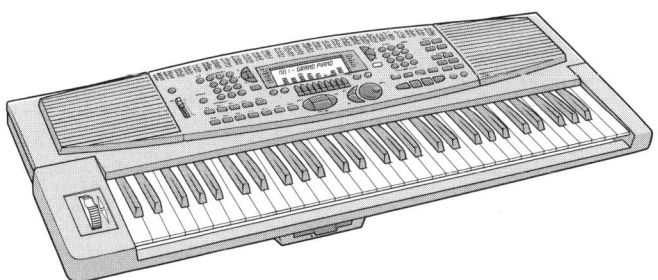

A home keyboard.

- A **sequential learner** prefers new material to be presented in a step-by-step fashion, and will be confused by a 'global' teacher who jumps from point to point without any apparent order. Likewise, those who prefer details will not as easily comprehend a teacher who presents a big picture perspective.

- **Graphomotoric learners** need to write things down to memorize them; this style can be applied to music too.

- **Intuitive learners** like the challenge of trying something new on their own, and they're not afraid to fail and try again. Non-

CHAPTER 2

intuitive or sensing learners prefer step-by-step guidance and support, avoiding surprises and experiments. Likewise, there are bandleaders who fire you if you make a mistake (non-intuitive), and those who fire you when you don't (intuitive): They simply have different interpretations of what it means to give your all.

Look at you
Tip: To define your child's learning style, it may be helpful to look at the way you like to learn things yourself, using the examples presented above.

3

Learning to Play

Is it hard to learn to play an instrument? No, not really. Almost anyone can, and almost anyone is able to play some easy pieces within a few weeks or months. And on the other hand: Yes, learning to play an instrument can be a daunting task. That is if you don't do it right, for example, or if you aim for the very highest level before you're ready. This chapter tells you everything you should know about learning to play an instrument.

CHAPTER 3

Playing the piano is no more than hitting the right keys at the right time, you could say. But it's also using your ten fingers to play infinite combinations of no less than eighty-eight keys. At the very same time you also have to listen to what you play (do I play the right notes in the right order, at the right tempo and the right volume?), and possibly to your fellow musicians, keeping one eye at the conductor and the other on your sheet music. That makes playing the piano sound fairly complex. Still, you (and your children) can master the instrument to some musical extent, just like you learn to drive a car, play computer games, and perform all kinds of other activities that are as complex as playing the piano.

Building a tower

Imagine being out in a field where lots of rocks are laying around, and you want to use those rocks to build a tower. At first, you make quick progress. Stones of all sizes are within easy reach, and piling up the first few feet is quickly done. Instant gratification! But the higher the tower gets, the harder things become and the slower they go. You have to climb all the way up to position new stones, and all the way down to get new building blocks — and you have to carry them all the way up, one by one. The higher the tower gets, the more time and energy this takes, and the harder it will be to balance things. But it's good that your tower gets higher too: you need it to spot more rocks in the area, required to get you to the next level.

Similar

Learning to play an instrument is quite similar. The first lessons are often very rewarding. Everything is new and exciting, and within weeks, children are likely to be able to play their first song, all by themselves. But as time goes by, learning an instrument turns out to be a process that gives its gratification only in the long term. You actually have to put in quite a lot of work before you move on to the next level of musicianship. There are long periods when progress seems slow or non-existent. These are the times when it can be really hard to keep on practicing. Why should you, when nothing happens? Truth is that things *do* happen, but very, very gradually, and they may take a long while to show. Knowing a bit about this process can help you guide your child through these periods.

LEARNING TO PLAY

> **No progress, still fun**
> To many musicians, progress — at any level — is essential to maintain an interest in making music and practicing. Still, millions of people enjoy playing at the same level for years and years. No towers to build, no stones to get; they just have fun at the level where they're at. Children can reach such a level within a few years of lessons (or even sooner) on any instrument.

Talent?

Some children can sing in tune at a very young age, implying they have a good ear for pitch. Others keep a steady beat early on, which suggests a good sense of rhythm. However, being talented in any musical way doesn't mean a child has the desire to learn an instrument. He or she may prefer to dance, or write, for example, or play ball. Conversely, many children who initially sounded horrible on the instruments they first tried, and acquired their basic musical competencies later in their childhood, have grown into successful professional musicians.

Bottom line

The bottom line? The talent or aptitude you may or may not spot in your children isn't that important. Don't let an apparent lack of it keep you from bringing music in their lives, and do not force your talented ones in directions they may not want to go in. First of all, let them have fun playing music.

WHAT YOU CAN DO YOURSELF

Children learn many basic skills in life by observing and imitating their parents. So why not include music? There are many things you can do to foster your child's musical development, and you don't need to be able to play yourself to do so.

CHAPTER 3

Sing
Singing to and with children is an easy, fun, and very effective way to educate them musically, and it's probably good for their verbal development as well. No matter how many different songs you present, be aware that your child will probably want you to repeat their favorite song again and again for a lengthy period of time, just like three- and four-year-olds may ask you to read them the same bedtime story for weeks on end. This is basically their first way to practice.

Old and new
Your child will learn all kinds of songs in special music programs, but also in school. Additionally, you can sing them the same old folk songs you grew up with: The good ones never seem to die. If you still need more music, there are numerous books with children's songs, either with or without sheet music.

Accompaniment
To find out what a new song should sound like, all you need is the ability to play the melody on a home keyboard with a single finger, which is something you can probably learn in a matter of weeks. Alternatively, there are CDs that provide you with professional accompaniment of numerous children's songs. All you and your child have to do is sing along. If you know the melody of a song, but can't remember all of the lyrics, simply search for the title online, or visit one of the available special lyrics websites. *Tip:* Learning the guitar to a point where you can accompany your children's songs isn't very hard either, and both acoustic guitars and home keyboards are affordable, yet valuable, investments.

Improvise
You can also make up songs yourself, singing about what you're having for dinner, or how fine your baby looks, or anything else that comes to mind. Use a familiar melody, or make one up yourself. There are no conditions other than having fun. Older children can be inspired to make up their own songs too, and some do so spontaneously, even three- or four-year-olds.

Call and response
Try singing call and response songs with your children. You sing

one or two lines, and they sing their response back to you, or you inspire them to repeat what you sang. With infants, try and see what happens if you respond to your baby's sounds by making those sounds back. It works!

Two, three, four
With most children's songs you know, you can simply count along in two (1, 2; 1, 2), three (1, 2, 3; 1, 2, 3) or four. (An example of a song in three would be 'My Bonnie Lies Over the Ocean', as shown below.) These so-called duple, triple, and quadruple meters are very common in Western music. Most pop songs are in four, as you can easily hear.

1 - 2	**1** - 2	**1** - 2	**1** - 2
Yan - kee	**Doo** - dle	**went** to	**town** -

1 - 2 - 3	**1** - 2 - 3	**1** - 2 - 3
My **Bon** - nie lies	**o** - ver the	**o** - cean -

Songs in duple meter (Yankee Doodle) and triple meter (My Bonnie).

Odd meters
Some music programs for children also include songs from other cultures. These songs may not have two, three or four beats to every bar, but five or seven, for example. This can be a bit confusing to adult Western ears, but children pick up such 'odd' meters very easily, as do the children of such cultures where these meters are anything but odd.

Action songs
Songs that invite children to move or dance, such as 'Itsy Bitsy Spider' or 'Head, Shoulders, Knees, and Toes', are very helpful for a child's rhythmical development. You can simply turn any song into a so-called 'action' song by clapping and tapping along with the beat, persuading your child to join you, or — when they're still too young — clap their hands for them. This teaches them how to keep a beat and helps develop their motor skills.

Dance
Dancing has a similar effect. Simply dance to the music (any music, really) with your baby in your arms, or dance with your

CHAPTER 3

child as soon as they can walk. You don't need to be a good dancer. Just move to the music. That's all there is to it.

Toy instruments
Get your child toy instruments. There is a wide range of child-safe, child-proof, and affordable musical toys available, ranging from pull-along animals that produce all kinds of sounds, to toy pianos, guitars, whistles, and so on. Toy percussion instruments (frame drums, bells, shakers, tambourines) are very accessible. Simply hitting or shaking them will do.

Play music
Play CDs or music radio stations at home rather than having the TV on 24/7. This will get children acquainted with and interested in music, and it will help their musical development through a process called osmosis: They absorb and learn about music without even knowing it.

All styles
There's absolutely no need to play children's songs only. Rather expose them to a variety of musical styles (and you may discover new horizons for yourself too!). Play them classical music, jazz, reggae, pop, soul, country, music from other cultures, and everything else that you think sounds good. There's also a lot of special age-appropriate music around that may please you as much as them. When children get a little older, you may want to ask them which styles of music they like best, and what it is they like about those styles. This helps to make them more aware of what they're listening to.

> **Instrumental music**
> As children tend to focus on a song's lyrics rather than the melody and rhythm, it's good to also play them instrumental music, such as most types of classical music or jazz. Music programs for young children often include age-appropriate instrumental music.

LEARNING TO PLAY

Repetition
Children may be very explicit when it comes to the type of music or the songs they like best. Allowing them to listen to certain songs time after time is much like the repetition of practice. Children who have their own audio player (CD, MP3, etc.) can select their own songs from the music you provide for them. Various companies make special players for kids. Some even include a microphone so your young one can sing along.

TV, CD, radio?
There are TV stations that broadcast only music, but getting your musical exposure from the TV is definitely a different experience than playing CDs, or listening to radio stations. TV's visual images can actually distract children from both the music and from engaging in concurrent activities such as playing, reading, or cleaning up their rooms. Plus, music TV stations generally play pop music primarily, whereas CDs and radio offer a much wider variety of styles to choose from.

> **Save money**
> Borrowing CDs in your local public library allows you to find out what you and your child like without spending a fortune buying albums. Alternatively, there are millions of songs and compositions available online. Please do respect the relevant copyright laws if you download music.

TIP

Learning by listening
If you play an instrument, listening to music is an essential way to improve your own playing. As children get older, they will definitely learn a lot (how to produce a great sound on the instrument, how to interpret and perform the music, and so on) by listening to others play — especially live.

Stay tuned
Once into their teens, children often develop new musical preferences. Just as often they grow to like a style of music that you don't like or understand, possibly the same way your parents felt

CHAPTER 3

about the music you liked when you were that age. Still, try to stay connected. Listen along with them or sit and watch their favorite clips on TV with them, assuming they let you. *Tip:* Some albums feature a 'Parental Advisory: Explicit Content' sticker. Note that bands or record companies are not obliged to state this warning, so you may want to keep an occasional ear on what your children are listening to.

Concerts

If you want your children to get the most out of listening to music, take them to concerts. Live concerts literally add life to the music, and watching people perform is different from simply listening to music at home or in the car. Also, taking your children to concerts teaches them to correlate the various sounds they hear to the specific instruments being used.

Tips

- A benefit of visiting outdoor concerts is that you can usually simply **leave before they're over**, should your child be bored.

- Look for special **music events for children**, organized by symphony orchestras or other organizations.

- Attending concerts can be an expensive activity, but there may be more **free or affordable concerts** in your area than you think, such as performances by college or high school bands, local church performances, and public festivals and events. Check your local newspaper!

EARLY CHILDHOOD MUSIC PROGRAMS

Music classes for the youngest are referred to as early childhood music programs, music education programs, or music readiness programs.

TIPBOOK MUSIC FOR KIDS AND TEENS

LEARNING TO PLAY

Fun
These programs typically help children to get actively involved with music in many different ways, from singing and playing musical games to moving to music and playing a variety of children's instruments, all in a very playful way. Some organizations also offer such classes for children up to ten years of age or older. Other programs offer subjects like ear training and ensemble playing, providing more of a solid foundation for further musical education.

Different groups
There are a number of different age ranges that these programs appeal to. Some offer classes for children from zero to eighteen months and eighteen months to three years; others have classes for zero to four-year-olds and four to seven-year-olds, for example. These age groupings are less relevant than the program's content, its underlying philosophy, and, most importantly, the people in charge. Your child should feel at ease with them, and they should be able to provide your child with a lot of fun — and music. *Tip:* Programs for the very young often invite or even require you to participate in the group's activities.

Music programs
Some of the better known, internationally available general music programs are Music Together, Kindermusik, and Music for Young Children. Two other names you are bound to come across are Orff Schulwerk and the Kodaly Method. Many music teachers who work with young children use elements of either or both of these methods. (See page 226 for websites.)

More sources

To find other music programs and methods online, search for the terms listed above (music education program, etc.), combined with your area code or city name. Alternatively, you may check with your local recreation and community service center, or with a community music school, for instance.

TIP

CHAPTER 3

Instrument-based programs

There are also instrument-based programs. The Suzuki Method, one of the best known programs, is used to teach violin, cello, piano, guitar, and other instruments to very young children. Parents join their children in these classes, and they have an active role in teaching them. They even get to play the instruments themselves. Children are taught to play pretty much the same way they learn to talk. Reading music is presented to the kids only after they have learned to play, just like you learn to read only once you have learned to speak.

The cello is a popular instrument among young children.

Teens too

Tip: Some teens and adults prefer learning this way too, and such courses are available.

Opponents

Not everyone agrees with the basic principle of the Suzuki Method. Opponents argue that learning to read may be difficult after learning to play, as it slows the learning process down at that time. Also, why would you need to read if you can readily pick up new songs by ear?

Costs

Exact prices for music readiness and early childhood programs depend on the type of program, as well as on where you live. In cities, things may be more expensive than in rural areas, and prices can vary per state or country as well. Most programs cost between some forty to eighty dollars a month, based on one lesson per week.

SCHOOL MUSIC PROGRAMS

Schools differ widely in the music programs they offer. This section offers an overview of what you may expect from school programs, and it offers information on what you can do if your child's school has few or no music resources.

Elementary school
Elementary schools may offer the following classes, either taught by a classroom teacher or, preferably, a certified music teacher.

- **Music exploratory programs** can include anything from singing and dancing to music appreciation, playing classroom instruments, and an introduction to composers, musical styles and instruments.
- Violin and other **orchestral string instrument lessons**. Some schools offer these programs as early as kindergarten.
- **Wind instrument lessons**.
- **Recorder lessons** typically start anywhere from 3rd to 5th grade.
- **Band and/or orchestra** usually start in 5th or 6th grade.
- **Chorus**.

Middle school, junior high
Many middle schools and junior high schools offer both band and orchestra. 'Band' refers to a concert band or wind band, two of the many names for a large ensemble that features a variety of wind and percussion instruments. Most school orchestras are comprised of orchestral string instruments only. (These and all other types of ensembles are explained in Chapter 8.) Separate music theory and music appreciation lessons may be available as well.

Keyboards, computers, and more
Schools that offer guitar and keyboard or piano classes are great for kids who are not interested in playing traditional band and orchestral instruments. Some schools also provide computers and music software, so students can learn to digitally compose and

CHAPTER 3

produce music. There are even elementary schools that teach third graders composition this way!

High school
High schools often have a variety of band programs, ranging from a concert band or symphonic band to a marching band, a jazz band, a pep band, perhaps even a mariachi band, or other types of bands. There are usually one or more choirs as well. Ideally, instrument and/or choral instruction is available for both beginners and advanced musicians.

College and university
Colleges and universities may have even more ensembles to choose from, especially if there's a faculty of music, of course. Ensembles may range from percussion ensembles and flute choirs to brass quintets and new music ensembles. These groups are not always open to all students; some are audition-based, others accept music majors only.

A professional career
If your child is considering music as a profession, consult their high school music teacher, band director, and guidance counselor about the possibilities for further education.

Universities and colleges
Professional education is available at a wide range of public and private universities, colleges, and a few independent conservatories or schools of music. Not all of these institutes cover all styles of music. Additionally, there are various examination boards that offer graded examinations for teachers and performers.

Other careers
A career in music doesn't mean a career as a musician or a music teacher per se. There are dozens of other musical careers, ranging from artist manager, film music editor, booking agent, composer or songwriter, and music business attorney to instrument maker, music librarian, producer, publisher, sound engineer, music critic, and so on. Note that some of the schools referred to above offer programs for students who want to specialize in audio

LEARNING TO PLAY

engineering, music business, songwriting, and other music-related areas.

Checklist
Before choosing a school for your child, consider the information on the previous pages as well as the following list.

- **Schools differ** in how much time is available for music instruction, rehearsals, and other musical activities. Some school bands rehearse no more than once a week; others play every other day.
- Have a look at the school's **auditorium** and music classrooms.
- What about the quality and condition of the **school's instruments**?
- Do music classes and rehearsals take place **during the day**, preferably right before or after school hours?
- Is **individual or small group instruction** available?
- Are there **specialized music teachers** on staff?
- Visit **school concerts**, or check out music contests sponsored by the school district. One of the best ways to judge a school's music education program is to see and hear its students play.

Pull-out lessons
Instrument instruction often takes place at the same time as other class periods, requiring that the student occasionally misses these lessons. Research suggests, however, that pull-out instruction

---

TIP

Parent-teacher association

If you want to be actively involved in the school's music program, consider joining a parent-teacher association or a parents-for-music organization. Such groups have committees that organize fund raisers (raising money for instruments, uniforms, and equipment), escort trips to performances, maintain uniforms, promote the band, and so on.

CHAPTER 3

sessions do not decrease a student's academic performance. On the contrary, music students consistently score higher on their SATs and ACTs. Nonetheless, if your child's academic performance is suffering because of pull-outs, try to arrange a rotating instruction schedule that prevents him or her from being pulled out of the same class each week.

NO MUSIC?

When school budgets are cut, fine arts programs are often the first to suffer. If your child's school does not provide music instruction as an integral part of the curriculum, you will have to take care of this part of your child's education by seeking private or group lessons elsewhere (see pages 36–40). This is not a bad solution per se. In many (European and other) countries around the world, school music instruction has always been limited to a maximum of one or two hours of music appreciation lessons a week. Instrument lessons, band, orchestra, and other musical activities are simply not considered part of the school curriculum. They're the parents' responsibility.

Music advocacy
Some schools manage to keep music programs alive regardless of budget cuts; others just cannot. As a parent, you can try to re-install music as an integral part of your child's school education: You can become a music education advocate and present the case for music in the schools to the school decision-makers. Various organizations provide you with all the information, materials, and tools necessary to be actively involved (see Music advocacy, pages 226–227).

Grants and instruments
There are organizations and programs that offer help by providing free music classes to elementary schools, or they present grants to schools for hiring music teachers or the purchase of instruments. Some examples are listed on page 229.

Music clubs
High school students can also take things in their own hands and start a music club, for example. Most school faculties will support such initiatives. The current teaching staff may even supply a music director. A local music store might offer a 'club discount' to members who buy or rent their gear exclusively from them. If there's a music college in the vicinity, its students may be willing to teach the members of the club at reduced rates.

No teachers
Reduced funding is not the only reason that schools cut or decrease musical activities. In some cases, there simply are no qualified teachers available. One solution may be to invite undergraduate college students to teach elementary and middle school students, or to involve them and other teachers in one of the many special programs aimed at cultivating and developing qualified teachers.

HOME-SCHOOL MUSIC PROGRAMS

Some one to two million US students are home-schooled, and this number is growing. If you want to enroll your home-schooled child in music lessons, look for a home-school music program in your area, either by checking the Internet or by contacting your local home-school support association. Such programs usually offer music theory and music appreciation classes as well as private and group instrumental lessons.

Yourself
Home-school music programs can be initiated by a music store, or by a group of home-schooling parents, for example. If you want to set up such a program, contact local music stores, churches, and educational institutions, and ask for their willingness to provide discounts, special rental programs, rehearsal rooms, instruments, instruction, as well as their knowledge and experience. Many successful programs have been launched this way. If funding is a

CHAPTER 3

problem, solicit music majors or retired music teachers who may be willing to teach or direct a band or orchestra.

INDEPENDENT INSTRUMENT LESSONS

If your children are serious about learning to play an instrument — or if you think this is an essential element of their education — their school instruction should probably be augmented with independent instrument lessons by a private teacher or community music school. Some middle schools and high schools have specialized music teachers who also give private lessons.

Special instruments
Oboe, bassoon, and French horn are often considered 'difficult' instruments to learn, and students who play them typically require additional private lessons. Without the extra instruction, students of these instruments often find it hard to keep up to speed with fellow student clarinetists, violinists, or trumpeters. That said, in the end every student will benefit from one-on-one instruction, and there's no one instrument harder than any other instrument, as discussed on pages 161–162.

Too much
Talented kids need private lessons to keep them interested and to ensure that their progress is not hampered by slower classmates. For slower students, private lessons can help them keep up with the rest of the band. However, taking both private and school music instruction can be too much of a good thing for some children, making them want to quit. If that happens, it's better to choose between the two and drop the other one, rather than risk having your child miss out on a music education. Less can be more.

Preferred instrument
In school music programs, children don't always get to decide which instrument they're going to play. If children want to play

a certain instrument, enroll them in private lessons before the school music program starts. This may help the band director decide to assign these children the instrument of their choice.

> **Late starters**
> For children who start their musical education much later, say in high school, private lessons can usually get them ready to join the school band in a matter of months.

GROUP LESSONS OR PRIVATE INSTRUCTION?

If you and your child have decided to go for additional instrument lessons, you may have to choose between small-group lessons and private instruction.

Group lessons? Yes!
While older and more advanced students will usually benefit most from private instruction, there are many things to be said for group lessons. Group lessons:

- can be **more fun**, as most children love to do things together;
- teach your child to be comfortable **playing when others** — besides the teacher or parents — are listening;
- show children that they're **not the only ones** who make mistakes;
- allow children to **learn from and with their peers**;
- teach them to **receive and provide feedback**;
- **save money**, as they cost less than individual lessons. (More on lesson prices on pages 42–43.)

Effective group lessons
For effective group lessons, the group should not be too large

CHAPTER 3

(usually three to four students; beginner groups in the early stages may be larger) and the lessons should be sufficiently long, i.e., half an hour at least. The teacher needs to be aware that the more gifted, more advanced, or harder-working students may be slowed down by the group, and vice versa.

Even faster
In a good, well-led group, students can even advance faster than they might do in individual lessons. The fact that they need to perform for and with others probably plays a role in this: The group provides an element of competition, which can be beneficial. No one wants to stay behind.

Group lessons? No!
There are things to be said against group lessons too, of course. For one thing, children do not learn and progress at the same speed. In a group, it is hard or even impossible to customize the lessons for each child and to adapt things to the individual needs of the children. Also, there will usually be less undivided attention paid to developing the many elements that make for good musicians. There are so many things students can do wrong, that it seems impossible to get more than one student to do everything right at the same time: the right notes, proper dynamics, good posture, breathing correctly, the right technique, accurate fingering, etc.

> **Your child**
>
> If your child doesn't seem to do well in a group, consider switching groups if possible, or opt for individual instruction after all. Solitary learners (see page 19) will likely be unhappy in a group, of course, and so will children who have problems handling negative feedback, especially in front of others. Yet, with a good teacher, the group setting may learn them how to deal with this.

Private lessons
As children progress and get older, a one-on-one learning situation is usually preferred by both students and teachers. Some students

are ready to switch from group to individual lessons after a couple of months; others do well in group lessons for a couple of years. This depends on the student, the group, the teacher, and possibly on the instrument as well. In the end, the personal attention of a private teacher is invaluable, and so is the fact that the lessons can be tailored to the individual needs of the student.

Both
Teachers may also combine group and individual lessons.

- Some teachers may offer both group and private lessons every week; others have students take an **occasional private lesson** to work on specific weak or strong points. (Even a single private lesson can result in remarkable progress!)
- In addition to private lessons, teachers may offer group lessons for **general subjects** such as music theory, or ear training.
- Another option is to **add short individual lessons** to each group lesson (e.g., student #1 before the lesson, student #2 after the lesson, student #3 before the lesson of the following week, and so on).

Family
A tip: Some teachers and schools offer heterogeneous instrumental classes, where students play a variety of instruments of the same family. The best known example would be a string class, with a mixture of violin, viola, cello, and double bass students. Such settings resemble an orchestral situation, and the ensemble may soon produce a fuller, more pleasing sound than a group of violin players only. Other experts, however, strongly disapprove of the idea of violinists teaching cello (and so on), stressing the differences rather than the similarities of these instruments — even for beginning students.

Vocal lessons
Individual vocal lessons usually aren't suggested before the age of ten, and many teachers don't accept students until they're twelve or older. Younger children usually learn singing in a group setting such as a children's choir or the school choir.

CHAPTER 3

> **TIP**
>
> **Boys**
> The transformation from a boy's voice to an adult male voice typically takes one to two years, between ages twelve and fifteen. In this period, boys often have a hard time controlling their vocal folds, which usually don't grow in accordance with the other parts of the developing vocal instrument. As a result, their voices leap from one register to the other. This involuntary yodeling may last quite a while. Some experts think its wise to postpone vocal lessons until the voice has 'settled'.

HOME STUDIOS AND MUSIC SCHOOLS

Many private instrumental and vocal teachers work by themselves, either from their home studio or out of a rented space in a local music store. Others may have formed a teacher's collective, and still others are employed by community music schools.

At home
Teachers with home teaching studios can be very flexible when it comes to scheduling and rescheduling lessons, for example, and you may be able to start lessons at any time of the year. Taking lessons in the comfort and privacy of a teacher's home may ease your child's anxiety, too. Home studio teachers are often completely independent. Others may be affiliated with organizations that provide structured music programs and support (such as training, educational materials, and advertising) for the teacher.

Music schools
A music school can be anything from an informal group of non-associated teachers who just happen to be renting a number of rooms in the same building, to an officially sanctioned

educational establishment with a clear philosophy, a wide variety of curricula, and a number of carefully selected, qualified teachers. Next to regular lessons, music schools may offer all kinds of extras such as:

- **ensembles** (orchestra, band, jazz bands, rock bands, choirs, etc.) and school concerts;
- band **coaching**;
- **extra classes** (ear training, music appreciation, etc.);
- **master classes** (taught by invited professionals and experts);
- **workshops** (for specific instruments, ensembles, styles of music, etc.);
- a **recording studio** and/or an auditorium;
- **programs for all ages**, from early childhood to teens to adults.

Community music schools

Community music schools are non-profit organizations that enroll students of all level. They're typically staffed with qualified teachers available at affordable rates, and usually have financial aid options available for low-income families. Community schools of the arts (see www.nationalguild.org, page 228) also provide dance, theater, media arts, and other classes.

LESSON TIMES AND FEES

How long do lessons last, and what do private lessons cost?

Half an hour

It is quite hard to make for an effective lesson in less than twenty minutes. Even for piano students (who don't need to unpack and tune their instrument), twenty minutes is often considered a minimum. Most private lessons last half an hour. Advanced players usually benefit from longer lessons, up to an hour or more.

CHAPTER 3

> **Twice a week**
> Half an hour can be too much for a young child's attention span. If so, you may consider two brief lessons per week (if your situation and the teacher of your choice allow this), with the added benefit that your child doesn't need to bridge an entire week between lessons. Conversely, older students may be better off with a longer lesson every two weeks.

Fees for private lessons

Prices for private lessons typically range from twenty to fifty dollars for one half-hour lesson on a weekly basis. The exact fee varies primarily according to where you live (cities are typically more expensive than rural areas) and the teacher's experience and qualifications. Low prices can be very attractive, but you wonder how qualified and effective a ten-dollar-an-hour music teacher can be.

A little extra

Many private teachers make house calls. In addition to the lesson, they may charge you for mileage and travel time. To save themselves from traveling more hours than they're actually teaching, they'll often state a maximum distance they're willing to travel. Be sure you're aware of these factors before choosing this option.

A little less

You may get a discount if you purchase a number of lessons at once, and teachers and music schools may offer a family plan (charging less for your second or third child). Also, some teachers are willing to negotiate their exact fee depending on your financial situation, and schools may have sliding-scale or low-income policies.

Save money

There are many other ways to save money on music lessons:

- Visit a non-profit **community music school**, or inquire if the school's music teacher also teaches privately.

LEARNING TO PLAY

- Find out if there are **music majors** in your area who are willing to teach (although an inexperienced teacher may not be the best choice for your child, even if it's cost-effective).
- Go for **group lessons** rather than private lessons (group lessons may cost as little as fifteen dollars for a weekly fifty minute lesson).
- See if it's possible to change from **weekly to biweekly lessons** (though this is generally not advisable for younger students).
- Find out if there are **scholarships** or other funding available from local service organizations, arts councils, or special programs. Band directors, music teachers, and teachers' associations and related organizations (see pages 228–229) should be able to advise you on where to find information. Some schools have scholarships available for private lessons.
- Singing or playing within a **church group** may offer some free instruction.

TEACHERS

The following sections offer helpful hints on how to find and assess a teacher, as well as notes on different teaching styles.

A side job?
Finding the right teacher for your children is crucial. Don't simply settle for the one next door just because they charge low fees and offer instructions on umpteen different instruments. Teaching music is about making children enjoy playing and practicing, and instilling a love for music that could last a lifetime. Such a task requires a good, dedicated teacher.

Seeking a teacher
There are many ways to find a teacher or a music school in your vicinity:

- Ask **friends**, family, and neighbors.

CHAPTER 3

- Consult with **school music teachers**; they often maintain lists of qualified private teachers.
- **High school music directors**, church music directors, the local orchestra (whose members often teach too), and the music department at your local college can also be good sources.
- **Music stores** may have teachers on staff. If not, they may be able to refer you to a number of teachers in the area.
- Contact your state's **music teachers association** (search online for 'music teachers association' and the name of your state), art councils, or your local recreation and community services department.
- A number of **special-interest websites** can help you find a teacher in your area. These databases usually offer a limited number of teachers only. Please see page 228 for examples.
- Using a generic **search engine** (search for 'piano teacher' and 'Long Beach' for example) can work, but such search strings may also produce irrelevant hits.
- Check **classified ads** in music magazines and local newspapers.
- Visit the public **library**, or contact the local chamber of commerce.
- Consult the *Yellow Pages* or similar sources.

GOOD TEACHERS

Anyone can refer to themselves as a music teacher. So how do you find a good one?

Rapport
A good teacher is genuinely interested in making your child enjoy music to the fullest, developing your child's art habit, and turning music into an inherent — and entertaining, relaxing, stimulating, exciting — part of his or her life. To do so, a teacher must be able

to establish a good rapport with your child. Children should feel perfectly safe and at ease with their teachers.

Enthusiasm

It's critical that teachers are not only able to convey music in a way that children understand, but that they also incite an enthusiasm and hunger for music. They also need to be able to make the children feel good about their musical performance, even at times when there's little or no progress (see page 22). A private instrumental or vocal teacher is often your child's only one-on-one tutor, so the quality of their relationship really counts. More often than not, these teachers become important role models for your offspring.

Long-term

The above implies that students preferably stay with the same private teacher for at least a couple of years. Changing teachers can slow a child's progress; kids may feel they have to start all over again, and new faces and habits may ruin carefully established musical routines. However, if children seem to dislike their teacher, if they have difficulties understanding them or don't seem to be inspired, changing instructors can prevent these students from quitting. There's much more on this sensitive subject in Chapter 5.

Good relationship

If a good relationship with their teacher has been established, children will be able to express their musical preferences and feel that they're being taken seriously. If the rapport between the teacher and student is open and trusting, a student can simply tell his or her teacher that they'll have less time for practice next week because of a school project, for example, without being embarrassed or upsetting anyone.

Learning styles

Good teachers know how to work with children with different learning styles and preferences. They can offer clearly structured lessons for those who need them, and offer other students more freedom and room for improvisation. They can explain things in either a step-by-step format or sketch the big picture, depending on the student's needs. Even so, keep in mind that student-teacher relationships are unique and personal. A teacher who does wonders with your first-born may be less successful with your second child.

All of you
A good instructor not only teaches children how to play an instrument, but also helps them discover how playing the instrument can make them feel better, raise their self-esteem, help them express their feelings, and so much more. In that sense, a music instructor teaches much more than the mechanics of hitting notes or strumming strings; they coach self-awareness and self-expression. Such teachers will also motivate your child to keep on playing when progress seems unnoticeable — and every musician, at every level, goes through that experience more than once, as discussed on page 22.

DIFFERENT TEACHERS

Just like all individuals, music teachers have different personalities, philosophies, methods, experiences, and ideas. Here are some random thoughts.

Answers or questions
In the old days, teachers used to tell you what to do, and that was basically it. Nowadays, most people favor teachers who tend to pose questions rather than simply provide answers. A teacher who inspires children to discover things for themselves is often more effective than someone who gives strict directives only. It's the difference between, 'Don't tighten those muscles!' and someone asking, 'Can you feel what happens if you relax those muscles?' It may also be the difference between an authoritarian, demanding, no-nonsense teacher and one with exceptional communication skills who feels music should be fun rather than produce high grades.

LEARNING TO PLAY

Because they care
That said, the latter can be just as demanding, and 'fun' teachers can scold and 'push' you to be a better player — not because they dislike you or want to be mean, but because they care and they can see your potential. A teacher who says you've done well when you know you didn't can be as detrimental and unmotivating as one who is never satisfied with your performance.

Frustration
A good teacher senses when students are frustrated (from playing music that is too difficult), or bored (from playing music that is unchallenging). That balance differs from student to student.

Assignments
Likewise, students can become frustrated because they get too many assignments, or bored if they get too few. Students should be able to accomplish the goal of each assignment in the time between lessons. Teachers should provide their students with progress checkpoints (e.g., being able to play the first sixteen bars after two days of practice, and the first thirty-two after five days), which help students measure their own small successes. These successes are great motivators.

Candy bar?
If your child wants to play the drums, anyone can teach him or her how to play a basic rock beat in a matter of days, offering instant gratification. But if children want to learn to master an instrument, rather than just learning to play a song, they'll need to be in it for the long haul. With a good teacher, they'll enjoy most of those years. Choosing teachers, in that sense, is like deciding what to give your children for breakfast: an instant gratification candy bar, or something nutritious that will serve them better in the long run? This doesn't mean that learning to play songs at an early stage is a bad thing. It is definitely one way to get them motivated past the tedium of playing scales exclusively.

Focus on music
In the end, however, music lessons should probably focus on music, not just on songs. It's true that taking lessons from a rock

CHAPTER 3

guitar teacher may help you become a great rock guitarist. But what if your interests shift to jazz later on? The best instructors teach you how to play the instrument, rather then telling you how to play a certain style of music. And even more than that, they teach *music*, allowing you to follow any musical path you want.

Show the other side
Students with a tendency towards perfectionism should perhaps not begin a new piece before conquering the first one, while students who are less into flawlessness and more into variety may quit if their teacher keeps them honing pieces they truly feel they're done with. That said, a good teacher will help the perfectionist see how counterproductive his of her meticulousness can be, and show the second student how rewarding it is to really master a song before moving on.

Student-centered teachers
Student-centered teachers tailor their lessons to their students' needs, preferences, limitations, talents, learning styles, and goals. This doesn't mean that they won't ask children to play pieces they don't like. After all, children often grow to like a piece once they can play it.

Method-centered teachers
For method-centered teachers, it's not the student but the method that prevails. They often use a set program that students have to match, providing clear-cut routes and goals so you (and your child) always know where you stand. This method can also be an advantage when students have to switch teachers because the program simply continues as before.

Listen
Good instructors teach their students not only to play, but to actively listen to music as well. (As such, students not only learn to appreciate music as an art form, but become more adept at hearing wrong notes and self-correcting when practicing.) They also teach their students how to produce a good tone and how to express themselves musically, rather than just executing the correct notes at the desired tempo.

... And more
Some teachers may also incorporate related subjects into their lessons, such as singing and movement (important primarily for younger children), music theory, ear training, improvisation, solo playing, and composition. Good teachers should also spend time on their students' posture, breathing technique, and all other elements that come into play when learning an instrument. They should also advise their students on how to plan and organize their practice sessions. (See pages 96–101 for tips on this particular subject.)

ASSESSING A TEACHER

Selecting the right teacher for your child often includes interviewing prospective teachers.

Who do you teach?
Many teachers accept any and all students, regardless of age, skill, or level. Others prefer to teach children exclusively. Some don't accept children under a certain age, or students who are just starting, or those who don't play well enough yet. Teachers also differ in what they demand of their students. Can children study with this teacher just for fun, or do they have to be diligent and prove their commitment and desire to learn?

Two or ten?
If you and your child are serious about learning to play an instrument, a specialized teacher — in addition to the school music teacher — will usually be the best choice. *Tip:* Some teachers indicate the level up to which they teach by listing their highest grade examination course taught, possibly even per instrument. See pages 66–69 for more information.

Good enough
Can a low-budget, used instrument in a bad state of repair be good enough to begin with? Yes, it can. But be aware that isn't likely to

CHAPTER 3

sustain your child beyond the early stages: It is probably good for the very first beginning, and that's it. You may want to keep this in mind when seeking a teacher too. You wouldn't let someone who simply happens to speak English teach your child how to write, so why would you let anyone who happens to play an instrument teach your child to play? (And as for teachers who claim they can make your child a star, ask yourself why these teachers aren't stars themselves…)

Qualifications

Most good, professional teachers have college, conservatory, or university credentials to support their experience with their instrument, or they have a teaching diploma from one of the recognized examination boards (see pages 67 and 227). Many are also certified by the Music Teachers National Association or a similar organization (see page 225).

Affiliations

Most teachers are also affiliated with one or more instrument-based organizations (e.g., National Flute Association, Percussive Arts Society), state-based organizations (e.g., Florida Music Educators Association), or national organizations (e.g., American Music Center, Chamber Music America). Not all of these organizations require their members to meet certain competencies or standards.

Great musician?

One's level of musicianship doesn't say too much about how proficient at teaching one is. There are phenomenal teachers who aren't great players, and great musicians who can't teach. You and your child may be better off with a moderate musician who loves

> **Special needs**
>
> Is your child a special learner? Find a teacher who knows how to deal with his or her special needs. Such instructors are available, even though their education may not have included specific training in this area. (See pages 65–66.)

to teach, rather than a great musician who teaches to makes some extra bucks. Some parents ask a prospective teacher to play a bit to see how their child responds; This is more about style, sound, and inspiration than assessing the quality of the teacher as a musician, of course.

Feedback
What about feedback on your child's progress? Some teachers provide you with a weekly report; others call you every month, and some wait for you to contact them. *Tip*: Establish the pattern of feedback that suits you, the instructor, and your child from the start.

Recitals and competitions
Ask prospective teachers whether they hold studio recitals as an opportunity for students to perform for parents, friends, family, and fellow students. If you believe that competitions (see page 71) or examinations (see page 69) are essential to a solid music education, find out if the teacher supports this philosophy and will help prepare your child for such events. Of course this requires the teacher to be familiar with relevant organizations, exam syllabi, etc.

Studio hours
The optimum lesson time for younger children is usually before 6:00 PM or on the weekends; for teenagers, lessons can also take place in the early evening. If you want to attend your child's lessons, times may be harder to schedule. For most children, it's best to have a standard lesson time, preferably with a teacher who is not frequently rescheduling lessons due to other obligations.

Studio policy
Most professional teachers have a written studio policy that lists rules regarding cancellations, rescheduling, payments, and so on. Ask for a copy and carefully read it before you commit. Should you avoid teachers who don't have a written policy? This may be an indication that you're dealing with an amateur, but there are great teachers who simply prefer a more organic approach to their business.

CHAPTER 3

Notebook

It's advantageous if your child has a notebook or lesson diary in which the teacher lists weekly assignments, provides short reports on their lessons and progress, and so on. Teachers may ask you to record your child's practice times in the notebook, or to sign the weekly assignments to ensure them that you're aware of and involved in your child's education. Some teachers also have their students use the notebook to comment on the pieces they're playing, or on how their practice sessions went.

> **TIP**
>
> **Website**
>
> As an alternative to the traditional paper notebook, a growing number of teachers provide their students with a website that can be used for everything listed above, as well as for sending additional instructions, asking and answering questions, sending reminders and other messages (lesson times, payment, etc.), listing practice tips, and so on.

Facilities

A teaching studio can be anything from a tiny cubicle in a music store to a spacious hall where an entire band could rehearse. Some have nothing but two chairs and a music stand, while others provide all the conveniences you could think of.

- Is there a **waiting room**, and can the restroom be used?

- For students who use the **house instrument** (piano, drums, etc.): Does the instrument seem in good repair and does the equipment look professional and up to date?

- **Can lessons be recorded** on audio or video for home reference (see page 54)? *Tip:* Some teachers also provide their students with accompaniment CDs, so they can play along with pre-recorded music.

- Are **teaching materials available** (method books, etc.)?

- Can you **park your car**?

LEARNING TO PLAY

GETTING THE MOST OUT OF LESSONS

To get the most out of lessons, an efficient practice routine is crucial. Pages 96–101 tell you everything you'd like to know on this specific subject. Here are some other tips.

Read
First of all, read the studio policy so you know when payment is due, what to do if a lesson needs to be rescheduled, or how to cancel if your child is ill and can't make it, etc. Most teachers and schools have a 24-hour cancellation policy: If you don't call at least twenty-four hours before the scheduled time, you'll have to pay for the unattended lesson. However, should something come up the day before the lesson, or at the very last minute, please do inform the teacher that your child won't be there, even if the lesson has been paid for — so the teacher isn't waiting (or worrying) needlessly. Do note that not all teachers and schools offer make-up lessons. Most that do require that make-up lessons occur within seven days of the absence.

Quitting
If your child wants to quit, most schools and teachers require you to inform them well in advance. Some schools and teachers charge you by the month (usually to be paid in advance), regardless of whether there are four or five weekly lessons in that month. If your child quits mid-month, you'll likely forfeit the money paid in advance. Again, do read the studio policy. If there's no written policy, ask the teacher about his or her rules on these and other matters. *Tip:* If a teacher cancels a 'fifth' lesson, they're usually not required to make it up.

On time
If children arrive late, teachers aren't required to extend the lesson time in order to give them the full session, so make sure your kids are on time. If there's no waiting area, try not to be there way too early either.

CHAPTER 3

Method books
If a teacher asks that your child obtain a method book or other materials, make sure your child can bring it at the next lesson. If a specific edition has been requested, don't substitute. Contact the teacher if you're having trouble finding the required edition.

Additional materials
Of course, you're free to purchase additional books and materials for your child, but it's usually best to consult the teacher before you do. Some books may be too difficult or too easy for your child at this time, or they may veer too far from the teacher's curriculum in other ways. Always inspire your children to play and to practice, but don't encourage them to do more than their teacher has asked.

The instrument
Try to ensure that your child's instrument is in good working order before every lesson, if possible. Replacing guitar strings or selecting another reed during the lesson time is a waste of valuable lesson time if these things could have been managed in advance. The same goes for tuning: If there's a waiting area, your child may be able to unpack, assemble, and tune the instrument before the lesson starts. *Tip*: the Tipbooks on musical instruments (see pages 239–243) offer plenty of advice in replacing strings, reeds, and other parts, as well as on tuning and assembly.

Recording the lesson
Recording the lessons allows your child to replay everything that was said and to review their own or their teacher's playing. There are various types of affordable recording devices available. For good results, you may want to invest in a portable digital recorder with built-in stereo microphones, available for less than a hundred dollars. Such devices can record hours of CD quality audio as well as MP3.

Attending lessons
Some teachers will happily invite you to your child's lessons; others prefer not to have you around, as a rule. Attending your child's first two or three lessons will give you an impression of what he or she is up to, and it will give you ample time to get to

know the teacher. Some parents attend the first or the last minutes of each lesson, so they are always up to date on their child's progress and assignments. Others attend every single lesson for the first half year or so. If you attend the lessons, see if the teacher is willing to let you have a go at the instrument yourself, allowing you to understand somewhat of your child's experience.

Be in touch
If the teacher doesn't contact you from time to time, you may want to stay in touch yourself to check you child's progress. Also, inform the teacher if your child has been unable to practice (due to sickness, school projects, or whatever), so the teacher knows what (not) to expect from your child. Also, it saves your child from the embarrassment of not being prepared.

Summer sessions
Academic progress doesn't seem to be hindered by a summer vacation, but if children don't attend music lessons for more than a couple of weeks, they will have a lot of catching up to do. So much, actually, that it may make them want to quit. After all, it can be quite frustrating to find out that you can't play the songs that you mastered before the summer holidays anymore. If your child's teacher doesn't teach during the summer months, you may want to encourage your child to participate in summer sessions or a music camp. (Search online for 'summer camp,' specifying the instrument, your state, and other relevant information, or ask the music teacher.)

> **One more**
> Not playing for a week or longer negatively affects wind instrument players more so than most other musicians. Returning to the instrument can readily produce sore lips and other unpleasant symptoms. The more a child normally plays, the faster the effect of not playing will be noticeable. Playing a long session right after a long break is a bad idea for all musicians, if they want to prevent blisters or painful fingers.

CHAPTER 3

WITHOUT A TEACHER

Countless people around the world have learned to play an instrument without any formal training whatsoever, including lots of professional and famous musicians (albeit outside of the classical world). Some instruments are better suited to self-instruction than others. Most self-taught musicians play guitar, bass guitar, drums, keyboard, or they sing — but you can learn to play the violin without a teacher too, should you really want to. The following section is mainly relevant for parents of teens.

So why?
If children want to play an instrument but refuse to attend lessons, you may try to persuade them with some of the following ideas.

- **Why re-invent the wheel** when there are so many people that are trained to help you? Go see a teacher once, just to get started, and then feel free to go back if you get stuck or don't progress. Teachers have been trained to show you the way out of ruts and around brick walls.

- There are teachers who can help you play **the music you want to play** without forcing you to learn things you don't want to learn, whether that's music theory, scales, or whatever. (Really good teachers will probably inspire his students to study those subjects in the end, as they will make them understand their relevance).

- If you teach yourself to play, you may end up **learning things the wrong way**. Bad habits won't get in your way at this stage, but as you progress, they can easily turn into serious obstacles. Also, ridding yourself of bad habits usually takes more time than getting things right from the start.

- **Teachers do much more** than simply demonstrate you how to hit the right notes (you may be able to do that yourself, after all). They also advise you on how to best utilize your strong points and how to deal with your weaknesses. And of course, they teach you to sound as good as you can.

- Lots of famous self-taught musicians eventually sought some **training from a teacher**!
- Have you ever met someone who was sorry that he had **studied with a good teacher**?

Books and DVDs

Can one learn to play an instrument from a book, an educational DVD, online demonstrations, or an interactive website? Surely, students can garner much from such media. The main problem, however, is the lack of personal feedback. Media provide information, no guidance. In other words, they cannot *teach* your child. The same goes for the learning tools that can be found on various home keyboards (e.g., built-in lights that indicate which key to play next). No matter how advanced and interactive these systems are, they can't replace a real live teacher. Also, using nothing but such media requires a lot of self-discipline, whereas a weekly visit to a teacher each week typically is a better way to keep students going (and practicing, and progressing).

What they can do

Books, DVDs, and the Internet can be very helpful, though — especially as an addition to lessons or if a student has had lessons in the past. *Tip:* Many well-known pop, rock, Latin, and jazz artists have their own instructional DVDs from which your child can study his or her favorite artist's style and technique at their own pace (provided your child's playing level is on par with the instructional material). Beware that not all of these DVDs are of great educational value, but your child may find them very inspirational.

Reading music

Teens would often rather not learn to read music, especially when their goal is to play drums, electric guitar, or bass in a garage band or a similar group. And truthfully, you can learn to play these instruments well enough to join a band much faster than you can learn to read music. Besides, as teenagers may tell you, many great songs have been composed by musicians who can't read a note. They're right. You can enjoy playing and even have a great musical career without reading music. So what can you tell your child?

CHAPTER 3

- Learning to read music is **not difficult at all***. Once you get the basics down (which a six-year-old can easily do, so why not you?) it's simply a matter of sticking with it; you'll get better automatically.

- Being able to read gives you instant **access to new music**. There are loads of books you can benefit from: books with great ideas for songs and solos, books with effective exercises, books in which your favorite musicians show you how they do it, and so on.

- It allows you to **play with musicians that you have never met before**. This also widens the range of gigs you can play, whether you're an amateur or a pro.

- If you can read music, **you can also write it**. If you get a great idea for a new song, solo, or exercise, writing it down is easier and more reliable than remembering it.

- You **won't be lost** if somebody asks you to play sixteenths

Chord diagram for guitar. Play string 3 at the first fret with your index finger, play string 5 at the second fret with your middle finger, and play string 4 at the second fret with your ring finger. The result is an E-major chord.

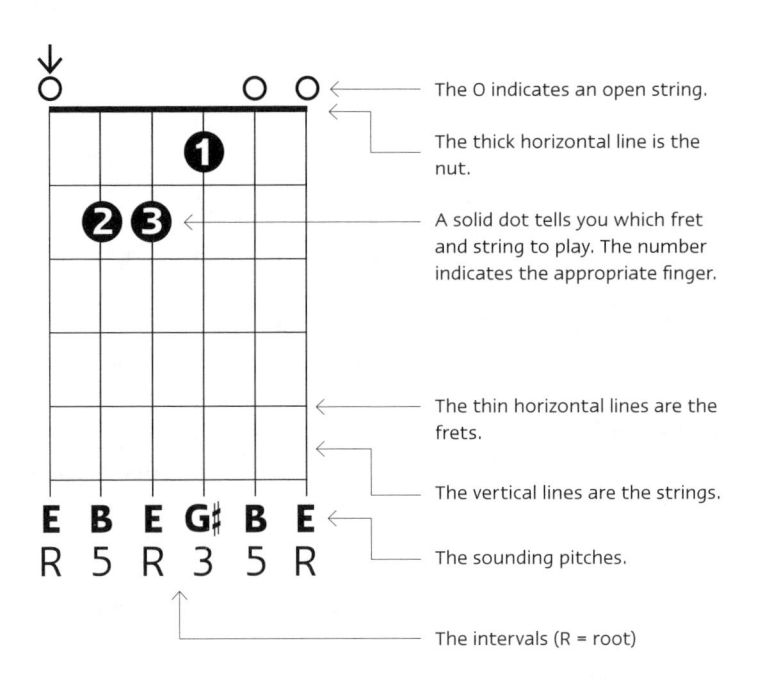

The 0 indicates an open string.

The thick horizontal line is the nut.

A solid dot tells you which fret and string to play. The number indicates the appropriate finger.

The thin horizontal lines are the frets.

The vertical lines are the strings.

E B E G♯ B E
R 5 R 3   5 R

The sounding pitches.

The intervals (R = root)

58

* Tipbook Music on Paper *makes learning how to read music really easy; see page 242.*

TIPBOOK MUSIC FOR KIDS AND TEENS

instead of eighths, or when your fellow musicians speak of diminished chords or flatted sevens.

- Realize that you can **forget about all those notes** once you start playing. That'll make you sound better too! (*Tip:* There's a section on memorizing music on pages 106–109.)

Chord diagrams and tablature

In addition to traditional music notation, there are various other ways to put music on paper. Guitar and keyboard chords can be represented by chord diagrams, guitar and bass solos can be shown in tablature, and similar notation systems exist for drums and other instruments. However, all of these alternatives have their limitations (e.g., tablature doesn't allow for exact rhythmic notation, and music is much more than just chords).

The numbers of the strings.

The strings   The fingers to use   The frets to play

The tablature staff represents a guitar neck.

DENTAL AFFAIRS: THE CHANGEOVER

If your child plays a wind instrument, will braces and the changeover from baby teeth to permanent teeth interfere with the learning process? Opinions differ. The good news is that many children actually become better musicians if they keep on playing with braces, or during their changeover. Opinions also differ when it comes to playing a wind instrument with baby teeth. For every teacher who is opposed to having children play wind instruments before they have their permanent teeth, you'll be able to find one who isn't, so the decision is basically up to you.

One-to-one

Whether it's about braces or playing a wind instrument before your child's permanent teeth have come in, one-to-one attention and personal guidance from a dedicated teacher is essential.

Better musicians?

One of the common errors children make when learning a wind instrument is that they apply too much pressure on the mouthpiece. This pressure causes the problems and pain associated with braces and the changeover. The solution is to simply minimize the pressure, which helps them become better musicians as an added benefit.

Clarinet, trumpet, flute

The most popular wind instruments for younger children are the clarinet (rather than the larger saxophone), the flute, the trumpet and the cornet, and the recorder. Can children play these and other wind instruments before they get their permanent teeth? Yes, they can, and numerous kids do and have done so without any problems whatsoever.

- To produce a pleasant tone and gain control of **the clarinet**, the player shouldn't bite or 'grip' the mouthpiece: Don't use the jaw muscles (the ones used for biting), but instead use the facial muscles surrounding the lips. After all, the clarinet can even be played by a person without front teeth! Can playing the clarinet push the front teeth outward? This seems to be unlikely, as this rarely even happens as a result of thumb sucking, and most toddlers spend more time sucking their thumbs than children do playing their instrument.

- The changeover can make **flute** playing a bit uncomfortable, but many children have sufficient control over their lips, which means they don't need the additional support of their front teeth.

- Things can be awkward for **trumpet and cornet** players, but a dedicated teacher can help them through this period. Problems can be prevented or reduced by selecting repertoire without high notes (e.g., the notes D5 and up, which demand extra pressure), or by adapting pieces with high notes.

LEARNING TO PLAY

- For the **recorder**, another woodwind instrument that's often played by youngsters, children should use lip pressure only.

- Most kids don't start on **oboe or bassoon** before they acquire their permanent teeth, simply because these instruments are too heavy and too large for them before that time. Down-sized versions do exist, however (see pages 155–156), and they're perfectly playable without front teeth or during the changeover.

A year from now?

None of the above means that problems won't occur, but if your child insists on a wind instrument, giving it a try is often better than telling him or her to wait for a year or two (as if they'd understand that concept anyway). Should the changeover cause more problems than your child can handle, then you might want to consider an alternative instrument for the time being, or forever. A break in a child's musical education can easily be for good.

DENTAL AFFAIRS: BRACES

Will braces keep your child from playing a wind instrument? In most cases, no. Will they cause initial discomfort and take some getting used to? Yes, they will. Some children actually have to give up playing because of their braces, and once they stop, there's no guarantee that they will return to it. So if your orthodontist advises that your child should not play a wind instrument at all, you may want to get a second opinion, preferably from a dental expert who loves music.

Flute? No! Yes!

While some children are advised to play the clarinet rather than the flute because of braces, others are told to play the flute rather than the clarinet — again, because of braces. Likewise, some say that braces should pose no problem for budding bassoon players, but there are some children who simply can't play this instrument with them. The truth is, the exact effect of braces on your child's playing depends on the combination of the type of braces, your

CHAPTER 3

... the flute, rather than the clarinet – or vice versa.

child's physiology, your child's instrument, and his or her playing experience. Experts' opinions differ, so make the decision based on your child's situation.

The problem
With most wind instruments, braces can induce pain as the insides of the lips are pressed against the braces' hooks and wires. Braces can actually cut your child's lips. (Using a medicated mouthwash to cleanse and disinfect those tiny injuries is not a bad idea.) Luckily, your child's lips will toughen up in time. Braces will also hurt a little every time they get adjusted, and each adjustment takes some getting used to. Finally, braces may cause an overabundance of saliva, which can hinder playing. This usually gets better over time.

The solution
Always inform your orthodontist of the instrument your child plays. He or she may be able to adjust the braces accordingly so they'll cause as little problems as possible. Having an orthodontist sensitive to and experienced with such needs — perhaps one who actually plays a wind instrument — helps. A tip: Some types of braces can simply be taken out when playing. If not, there are several ways to reduce the discomfort of the braces' sharp points. These are discussed on pages 63–64.

Flutists
One of the biggest problems for flutists is that braces may change the critical position of their lips. This can alter the sound, making it a bit thin, misty, or fuzzy. Each type of braces causes a different effect, but, under the guidance of a good teacher, these effects can all be dealt with. The adjustment usually takes from a couple of days to a few weeks. Lower braces can be a bit more troublesome than upper braces, as the flute rests against the lower lip. If

braces are hindering the air stream, try making the lip plate a little thicker by sticking one or more pieces of duct tape or masking tape on the lower part.

Clarinetists and saxophonists
Braces can be painful for clarinetists and saxophonists as well, and they can induce a fuzzy, airy tone at first. Adjustment often takes two weeks to a month. Braces usually hurt more as you clench your jaws more, which you shouldn't do anyway. *Tip:* Changing the angle of the instrument may ease the discomfort.

Brass players
For brass players, it may take longer to adjust, as they have to learn to minimize the pressure of the instrument against their lips, which will make playing high notes hard at first. If the braces really hurt, teachers may select a repertoire without high notes, or make adjustments to such sections. Using a mouthpiece with a wider rim (distributing the pressure over a larger surface) may help. Instruments with small mouthpieces (e.g., trumpet, cornet, French horn) typically cause more problems than the brass instruments with larger mouthpieces, such as trombones or baritones. Some kids do switch to another brasswind to solve the problem.

Oboists and bassoonists
For oboists and bassoonists, the discomfort of braces can be eased by using a lighter reed, which reduces the pressure on the lips. Lighter reeds will make for a thinner, more piercing sound, but that's a small price to pay. Most players will get used to their braces in two weeks or so.

Tissue, wax, and more
There are several other ways to reduce the discomfort caused by the many hooks and wires of braces.

- A readily available **stopgap solution** is to line the braces with tissue.
- Ask the orthodontist for a **special wax stick**. Rubbing the wax along the braces will cover the sharp points.

CHAPTER 3

- As an alternative, there are various types of **commercially available bumper guards**, caps or cushions that cover the braces, and a system that allows you to custom-make your own brace cover. Products to check out include Brace Guard Lip Protector, Morgan Bumpers, and the Jet-Tone Lip Protector. Note that guards and covers that add too much mass to the braces may reduce the players' control over their lips.

- *Tip:* Tell your child to **stop practicing when it hurts**. Take things easy, and accept that progress may slow down for a while. A bit of extra personal guidance can be essential.

When they come off
Children should be prepared for another potential adjustment period when their braces come off. Sometimes the loss of braces takes more time to get used to than getting them. Tip: There are a number of special exercises that help your lips get back in shape as soon as possible. Ask your teacher for help.

CHILDREN WITH SPECIAL NEEDS

There are trumpet players who were born with a cleft lip and palate, professional musicians with profound hearing loss, and severely disabled keyboard players who press the keys with their tongue... Children who really want to play music are able to overcome pretty much any type of disability. (There's a short section on physical impairments and choosing an instrument on page 151.)

Hearing impairment
Children with a serious hearing impairment can learn to enjoy music by feeling the vibrations. Some can even tune their instrument via these vibrations. Many of them can join the school band or orchestra, as they can rely on watching the conductor and

their fellow musicians, rather than listening, to know when to stop or start. Also, there are signing choirs for the hearing impaired, performing everything from Broadway hits to rock songs.

Visual impairment
Because they usually can't read music, visually impaired children often learn to play by ear, memorizing the music, and improvisation. In other words, they will usually play rock, pop, folk, jazz, or related styles, rather than classical music. Do note, however, that classical music is available in Braille —and you may find Braille notation in other styles of music as well.

Dyslexic children
There are various degrees of dyslexia. Given time, dyslexic children can typically learn to read music, just like they can learn to read text. There are plenty of dyslexic music teachers to prove this. Sight-reading (reading the notes of a piece as you play) will often be impossible, however.

Note names
For dyslexic children, the note *names* (C, D, E, F, G, A, B) may be harder to read than traditional music notation. After all, if you reverse the image of a note, as dyslexic children often do with letters, it is still the same note! There may be other problems, however, such as interchanging the left and right hand piano parts.

Playing by ear
Like visually impaired children, children with severe dyslexia may be better off learning to play by ear, and studying jazz, rock, pop or similar styles rather than classical music. *Tip:* Reading music while listening to a performance of the piece may be very helpful. An even more important tip: If you have a dyslexic child, consult a dyslexia specialist if playing or reading music seems troublesome, and you may even want to see if you can find a music teacher who has worked with dyslexic students before.

Mentally challenged children
Mentally challenged children often respond very strongly to music. Numerous musical games and programs have been

developed to help them connect with others, guide their social behavior, and reach their inner worlds. Likewise, autistic children can benefit from specific musical group activities. The musical performance of mentally challenged individuals often equals that of other children of the same mental age, and individual instruments lessons can provide them with great joy.

Learning impaired children

Unfortunately, most music education programs don't include courses on teaching children with learning (or any other) disabilities, even though an estimated thirty to forty percent of all children fall into this category to some degree. This high percentage indicates the importance of finding a teacher who really relates to your child and brings out the best in them. Some teachers attend special courses on working with impaired children, while some simply have a natural talent for doing so.

Gifted children

Gifted children have special needs too. More often than not, they have exceptional abilities in more than one area. Should that not include music, playing in an ensemble can make a gifted child feel as though they belong to a group — moreso than they often do elsewhere. If music is one of your child's special abilities, and a musical career is being considered, it's good to know that there are special schools, accelerated classes, and specialized teachers at your child's disposal. Associations for Gifted Children will offer further information.

EXAMS AND COMPETITIONS

In many countries, music exams have been a highly valued part of every child's musical education for generations. In countries where this isn't the case, however, the quality of music education hasn't seemed to suffer. What kind of exams and grading systems are there, what are the pros and cons, and what about participating in individual competitions?

Instrument graded exams

There are various organizations that offer graded examinations on instruments. Unfortunately, there is no internationally standardized grading system, as you will see below. Some organizations may recognize certain examinations, but not others, and transfer credits are usually not offered. Websites of the following organizations can be found on page 227.

- Exams of the Associated Board of the Royal Schools of Music (ABRSM) can be taken in **more than ninety countries**. Grades 1 to 3 are for elementary players; 4 and 5 are for intermediate players, and 6–8 for advanced musicians. There's a Prep Test at a pre-Grade 1 level for the very youngest, and the ABRSM has exams for professionals as well.

- The **Canadian** Royal Conservatory of Music (RCM) has similar examinations, but their grading system is different (1, intermediate; 5–7, late intermediate; 8–10, advanced). Preparatory A and B are for beginners in their first two years. In the US, RCM examinations are offered under the name of Royal American Conservatory Examinations. The RCM has exams for teachers' and performers' diplomas too.

- **Conservatory Canada** offers gradation similar to the RCM; CC allows you to take all of your exams on popular material (e.g. jazz, latin, contemporary).

- Trinity-Guildhall (UK) was the first international examinations board.

- In **Australia** and **New Zealand**, examinations are offered by the Australian Music Examinations Board (AMEB) and Australian and New Zealand Cultural Arts Limited (ANZCA).

- The Yamaha Music Education and Examination System has received international recognition in more than **forty countries**. Their grading system starts at Grades 13–10 for beginners; Grades 2 and 1 are their concert artist awards.

- The **New York-based** NYSSMA grades music from 1, very easy, through to 6, very difficult. Level 6+ pieces can be played by very advanced players and pros only.

CHAPTER 3

Other organizations use a letter system rather than figures, 'A' usually being the highest level.

What?
The exact requirements for each grade are listed in a syllabus that is available through the examination board. Exams usually consist of the following parts:

- Playing one or more **prepared pieces** (usually to be chosen from a repertoire list of required works) and a number of scales and or arpeggios.

- **Sight-reading**.

- **Aural tests**, such as identifying scales, chords, or intervals by ear.

Which grade?
There's no need to start with Grade 1. If the teacher feels your child is ready for Grade 4, he or she can usually take that exam right away. Of course, the teacher needs to be familiar with the requirements of the examination board. *Tip:* Exams are usually open for everyone, regardless of age and previously passed exams, and whether you have a teacher or not. It follows that you can also skip grades.

When?
What level 'Grade 4' or 'Grade 8' is, exactly, depends on the examination board, as indicated above. As a guideline, the average age range of RCM Grade 10 or the generally equivalent ABRSM grade 8 candidates is sixteen to eighteen. Students often pass one grade per year, but you can also pass two, or you can take your next grade after two or more years of study: Exams can usually be taken throughout the year. Ideally, students take exams when they and their teachers think they're ready, and not because a certain period of time has passed or because it happens to be that time of year.

Theory
There are theory exams as well. Some boards require that you have passed, say, their Grade 5 Theory of Music before you can take

LEARNING TO PLAY

Grades 6, 7, or 8 Practical on your instrument. Other boards let you take any grade without a proven knowledge of theory, as they believe that practical grades are about evaluating a performance only.

Milestones or hurdles?
Experts often see exams as milestones that gauge a student's progress, or as essential stepping-stones in the learning process, providing students with a specific goal to focus on, thus inspiring them to practice. Knowing where you're going can definitely make you work harder. Others consider exams as hurdles in the learning process, disrupting the student's natural progress. Yet, there are students who like jumping hurdles… Here are some random thoughts on the pros and cons of taking exams.

Pros

- Taking an exam is a **reward** for having practiced diligently.
- Passing an exam often **makes students proud** of what they've achieved, inspiring them to move on.
- Taking exams provides students with **helpful comments** from someone other than their teacher.
- Passing a grade may help a student **get into a band** or orchestra.
- Having a framed, graded certificate on the wall is **physical evidence** of a student's hard work.
- Many students are **challenged by exams** and love taking them.
- Exams offer a **performance opportunity**.
- A syllabus provides students and teachers with a clearly **structured educational program** so students know exactly what is expected of them.
- Exams and grades introduce an element of **competition** into the music.

Cons

- Music is about having fun and enjoying yourself, not about taking exams. **Exams are scary.**

CHAPTER 3

- An exam can easily turn into a goal in and of itself, becoming the **sole purpose of practicing** rather than something to pass by as the student progresses.

- Being able to perform **well on an exam** does not automatically mean that a student is able to perform well in front of an audience.

- Exams make students focus too much on **required pieces** (and perfect them until they're no fun to play anymore), rather than inspiring them to explore other repertoires as well.

- Many children will never get beyond a certain level. The obligation to take exams will confront them with their limited abilities and **make them want to stop**, while they could have enjoyed making music for the rest of their lives.

- If a teacher provides students with proper feedback and encouragement, there's **no need for exams** to prove they're progressing.

- Exams offer a performance opportunity — but who needs a performance in which **you can fail**?

- (Most) exams don't test how you **perform in a band** or an orchestra.

- Exams can make or break a student's **confidence**.

- Exams and grades introduce an element of **competition** into the music.

TIP

Scary
Are exams scary? Not if you love taking them. For others, they always will be, even though board examiners are expected to make accommodations in order to reduce fear, and to encourage candidates to play to the best of their abilities. To help young students get used to taking exams, there are special exams that they can't fail. Chapter 10 has tips to deal with or reduce exam nerves.

Required exams
If your child doesn't like jumping hurdles (and if you don't think that should be changed), you'd probably better not send him to a school that requires taking exams to pass to a next level. Taking exams can work well for many, but they're not essential for a fruitful musical education, as millions of musicians can testify.

Fees
For information on exam fees, see page 139.

COMPETITIONS

Besides band competitions, there are all kinds of competitions for individual musicians. Some are intended to select musicians for an ensemble or a school, for example. Others offer a monetary prize for the winner exclusively. Some present all participants with no more than score sheets and constructive comments from the jury, and others have prizes for all contestants, turning the event into a positive experience for all.

Pros and cons
Most of the pros and cons of taking exams also go for participating in competitions. Children get to play for and be judged by persons other than their teacher, which may be very enlightening as long as the feedback they get is strictly constructive. At a competition, children will meet other students who are often just as nervous as they are (which may be a consolation, but it can also make things even worse), and what they hear other children play may inspire them to play even better — or frustrate them so much that they want to quit right away. What to do? Have a good look at your child and seriously talk things over, trying to figure out what seems best for him or her. You may also consult their music teacher, or simply inspire you child to give it a shot and see what happens before, during, and after the event. A tip: Some children participate in competitions to get used to playing in front of judges so that taking an exam becomes a less fearful event!

CHAPTER 3

The teacher
Teachers should be able to properly judge their students' levels before enlisting them in a competition or exam. This prevents students from experiencing unnecessary frustration and failure.

Band competitions
For drum corps and various other types of bands, competing is a major part of the musical experience. There's more about these and other types of bands in Chapter 8.

Practicing

Many children don't like to practice, and the same goes for many adults, and even for some professional musicians. Why? Because they want to play their favorite music, rather than spending hours playing scales, etudes, or arpeggios. Because, oftentimes, progress doesn't show right away. Because learning to play an instrument is about long-term gratification, and we seem to have lost touch with that concept. Or because of any other reason... But still, it needs to be done, and it can be entertaining, too!

CHAPTER 4

This chapter offers helpful hints on how to practice efficiently, turning it to a rewarding and inspiring pastime. Ineffective practice habits are as much work as effective ones, but yield no progress and may cause children (and adults, again) to quit playing. Also included is vital information on where and when to practice, the various ingredients of a good practice session and how to structure it, practice techniques, memorizing music, and much more. Having some insight in these matters will make it easier for you to guide your children in this essential part of their music education.

Sports
Practicing is to music what training is to sports, but there are some major differences. Firstly, most sportsmen train with their teammates, while practicing is something you usually do alone. Secondly, if you play football, baseball, or any other type of sports, you'll probably have a match every week. Most musicians don't have that many opportunities to perform — and usually, being able to perform is why you practice in the first place.

Joining a band
That's why it's important for kids to join a band or an orchestra. It offers performance opportunities, it's a great way to meet new friends, and it provides your children with clear and realistic goals. Practicing so you can play your part at the next rehearsal is a better motivation than practicing simply because you're supposed to.

One note
Joining an ensemble is even more important for children who play violin, cello, flute, saxophone, or any of the other instruments that typically produce one note at the time. These single-note instruments or melody instruments are best suited for group settings. If there's no such opportunity, you can also arrange for your child to play duets with a friend, or a fellow student of his teacher: There are plenty of works for two violins, two flutes, flute and piano, and other duos.

Chords
It's a bit different if you play the piano, guitar, keyboard, or another chord instrument. These instruments allow you to

PRACTICING

play both a melody and chords (three or more notes at once), so you're effectively providing your own accompaniment. As a result, practicing on one of these instruments is musically more rewarding than playing a melody instrument on your own.

Keep on going
It's clear that practice is necessary to achieve a certain level. But should children continue to practice once they've reached a level they're satisfied with? Maybe not, if they're at a point where they can perform at a level that satisfies them. (Note that they'll still get better as they keep playing their instrument.) Unfortunately, many kids who stop practicing will soon find themselves restricted to playing the same pieces again and again. If boredom sets in, the end of their musical endeavors may be near.

No practicing
So can you play without practicing? Of course you can. There are many garage band musicians who never practice. They just play with their friends, and they're having a ball doing so. However, they will usually stop playing once they get a little older. Having no real musical foundation, it's quite unlikely that they'll pick up an instrument again later on in life.

Recreational music making
Participating in a drum circle, for example, allows anyone to play music with a group of people without any prior experience. These and other recreational music-making activities are about socializing, reducing stress, and relaxation more than about striving for musical prowess. (Incidentally, that's what most garage bands are about, too.)

Not another obligation
For children who want to pursue a career in music, their practice habits should foster diligence, hard work, and making sacrifices, though the latter may not be considered as such. For all other children, practicing should be more about fun and less of an obligation, as pressure and taking things too seriously can make the fun go away. But what if they don't want to practice? Shouldn't you exert at least a little pressure?

CHAPTER 4

Means, goal, or making music?
Practice can be considered a goal in and of itself, and that goal is achieved by practicing, say, half an hour a day. Others see practice as a means to an end, the end usually being the ability to play well, at whatever level, and to perform successfully. You can also consider practice as making music, as a journey that leads to who knows where, and the journey itself is what it's all about. For students who have teachers whose assignments (both in quantity as in quality) inspire them to play, and who get them to really understand why playing scales or practicing rudiments is essential (because that understanding usually makes this part of practice less of a drag), there may be no need for pressure. The more a student considers practicing to be a goal in itself, the more pressure you may need to apply to keep them practicing. That said, almost every child needs to be pushed a little from time to time.

HOW LONG — OR HOW?

One of the most frequently asked questions is, 'How long should my child practice?' But wouldn't it be more interesting to look at what should or could be achieved, rather than at a set number of minutes? That way, the student's focus would be on accomplishing a particular task, rather than on simply filling time. Still, no matter how you look at it, a child must invest time in practice, and it's essential to be able to gauge how much time that typically is.

Three to six
Most experts seem to agree that you can't really speak of 'practicing' when kids are three to six years of age. For this age group, it's more about spending quality time and having fun with the instrument (if they've actually already chosen one) than about trying to achieve something other than a long-lasting love for music. For most of these children, playing up to five or ten minutes a day will be fine. The shorter these sessions last and the more fun they are, the more likely your child will want to play three, four, or more days per week.

PRACTICING

Six and up
As children get a little older, they'll be able to focus for longer periods, and they'll start to grasp the concept of doing things now that will pay off later. They will also be ready to maintain a practice routine with their teacher's and your guidance. Six- to eight-year-olds should typically spend some fifteen minutes per day on an instrument, for anywhere from four to six days per week. As they get older, they will usually be able and willing to play longer. Many children are expected to play about a half an hour a day or more. If they practice effectively, however, they may be able to do their assignments in less time — which can be so rewarding that they end up playing longer!

> **Short and often**
> A half hour practice session can easily be too long, so it's often better to divide the routine up into three ten-minute sessions, or even six sessions of five minutes each. Short sessions tend to be more effective, with improved retention and more focus.

Much longer
The better your children get at playing their instrument, the more they need to practice to progress and maintain their abilities at a desired level. Music majors often practice three to five hours a day. The longer they practice, the sooner they will find that not practicing seriously slows them down or affects their playing in any other way — so they have to keep up all, or most, of the time!

Music, not minutes
For students to focus on the music rather than the minutes passing by, they must understand exactly what their teacher expects, and they must be able to self-assess whether they've achieved the goals set for the next lesson. This requires teachers to be very explicit about their assignments. For example, rather than simply telling a student to 'learn to play that piece,' teachers should state specific criteria, (i.e., 'play it with the metronome at 116 beats per minute,'

CHAPTER 4

or 'play these scales five times, without any mistakes, at 138 beats per minute'). This way, students can simply tell when they've completed the assignment.

More than a routine

If a teacher is able to convey the practice techniques that help the student to most effectively reach the goals set for that week, practicing can be much more than a thirty-minute routine to be endured. It also puts things into the students' own hands: If they practice efficiently, it'll take them less time; and if it takes them less time, they can even decide to take a day off — or, even better, they might be inspired to do more than they were asked to in the first place.

Your own teacher

Practicing is something that needs to be learned (and taught). When children practice alone, they're expected to catch their own mistakes, to discover what prompted these mistakes, to fix them, and to find a way to prevent them in the future. In effect, when practicing this way, children are their own teachers — which is not easy.

> **At home**
>
> When kids get to their next lesson, they sometimes find out that they're not able to play what they could play at home. Or could they? Did they really hear everything that went wrong? Did they repeat everything to a point where they could even play it under pressure? Probably not. Playing in front of a teacher, or anyone else, including you, is quite different from playing when no one is around. That's why it's good to ask your children to play for you every now and then, at the end of their practice session, or perhaps as a weekly routine. Getting experienced in how to play for others is an important part of the learning process.

WHEN

Ideally, practicing should become a daily routine; something as natural as having dinner or brushing your teeth. And just like most people have dinner or brush their teeth around the same time every day, practicing is more likely to become a natural part of the day when it's done at or around a set time. Getting children used to spending some time with their instrument on a regular basis may be more important than how much practice they actually do, initially.

Every day?
Should children practice every day? It's unlikely that anything you *have* to do seven days a week will be a lot of fun. That's why most experts state that five to six days a week will be sufficient to make progress. With one lesson and five days of practice, your child is still playing six days a week.

Which day?
Sunday is the day of the week that's most likely to be your child's preferred day off, but you may point out that this day allows for more time to practice than most other days in the week, and that practicing still leaves plenty of time for other activities. You can also leave it up to your children to pick their day off per week.

> **(Not) making it up**
> Should kids occasionally miss any of the other days, you may consider not asking them to make it up. Skipping a day now and then is no disaster. You may try to inspire children to practice a little more the day before their 'extra' day off, however. Tip: The day before the lesson is usually the worst one to skip practicing.

A closer look
It's often very effective to have a short practice session right after the lesson or later that same day. This reinforces the lesson

CHAPTER 4

content, and it's a perfect opportunity for you and your child to take a look at the weekly assignments. Be around, if possible, and make sure your child understands everything he or she has to do that week. If anything is unclear, you or your child can get in touch with the teacher to clear things up.

No time?
On days that are too busy to do the entire practice routine, you may suggest children to just play one of their favorite pieces, or something else they like play, as long as they keep in touch with the instrument. A tip: Suggest them to play for just two or maybe three minutes. They may very well end up playing longer!

When?
Many kids like the security of practicing at a set time or moment of the day (before school, right after school, or before dinner, etc.), especially when they're too young to know how to schedule their time. Others prefer to schedule their practice time around other obligations. That way, they can play when they feel like it, rather than having to do so because it happens to be 4:00 PM. Here are some additional tips on planning practice sessions:

- Practicing before doing homework provides a **fun break** between your child's academic activities, but it may be hard to focus on music if there's a lot of homework to be done.

- Practicing after homework (one obligation after the other) can make children feel as if they're **never done**.

- Some kids love to practice **before going to school**.

- Planning a practice session **before their favorite TV show** (which then turns into their reward for practicing) may be more successful than asking them to play after that show.

- If weekday practice sessions are prompted by your child's school day schedule — for example, practicing before or after school — then make sure he or she has **practice cues for weekends** and holidays as well (after breakfast, before dinner, etc.).

- If there's more than one child at home, have each one practice **while the others** do their homework (provided the musicians don't disturb their siblings). Playing scales when you know your sister is watching TV or chatting is usually harder than when you realize she's doing math.

Holidays

It's really important that children keep to their practice routines during school holidays. If they don't touch their instrument for three or more weeks, the first lessons and practice sessions after the holiday will most likely be highly frustrating as children probably won't be able to play those same pieces anymore. You may consider negotiating a holiday schedule with them: for example, playing four instead of six days a week, or suggest that they practice first-thing after breakfast, leaving the rest of their day wide open. This is a great practice time for weekends too!

How?

Children have their own ways of handling assignments, most likely approaching them the same way they do other things in life. Teachers should recognize these individual styles and help students to apply their way of handling things to their practice sessions, making these sessions as efficient as possible. Some examples:

- Children who're not good at **focusing their attention** should not be assigned three new pieces at once.

- Children who are **afraid to start a new piece** may tend to 'practice' pieces they already play very well. They're dedicating time to practicing, but without progress.

- Children who aren't aware of their own mistakes will end up **rehearsing those mistakes**, and it'll be hard to reverse and 'deprogram' the errors. These students need to learn how to evaluate their own playing before moving on.

- Children who **skip sections** they can't play should be treated differently than those who keep repeating things without getting any further.

Discuss

If you feel that your child's practice habits aren't as fruitful as they could be, or if you notice that any of the problems mentioned

CHAPTER 4

above are occurring frequently, you should discuss how to handle this with his or her music teacher.

Sitting in

Do you need to be around when your child is practicing? Young children often don't like being alone when they play. Just being there might be comforting to them (as long as you're not distracting them); so read a book, or pay the bills, for example. Children may also appreciate it if you're actively involved — so sit with them, listen to every note they play, read along with the music, and help them out when they get stuck. It is unrealistic to expect children under the age of ten to plan, organize, and maintain an effective practice routine.

Progress

If you simply want to keep an eye on your child's progress, you might just join them for a couple of minutes of each practice session. Recurrent recitals, as discussed on page 99, are good ways to keep in the loop, but it might be better to actually watch your child practice, from time to time. You'll learn how they manage their time, tackle problems, and so on. This can also be a valuable source of information for their teacher. If your child doesn't like having you around during practice time, simply leave him or her alone. In most homes, you will still be able to hear how things are going.

> **Judge**
> If a teacher specifies that your child should be able to play a particular piece or etude by the end of the week, it may be up to you to assess whether or not that goal has been achieved. As children mature they will hopefully develop the ability to evaluate their own playing. Tip: Suggest to your children that they record themselves playing the assigned piece, and then ask them to use the recording to judge their performance. This is very instructive for musicians at any level. (There's more on this on page 213.)

82

TIPBOOK MUSIC FOR KIDS AND TEENS

PRACTICING

WHERE

Ideally, children should be able to practice at any time of the day, without being hindered and without hindering others (see page 89). A practice space can be any room in the house. Preferably, it's a room where children can play their instrument with no-one around. If it's possible to leave the instrument unpacked between practice sessions, no valuable time (or inspiration) gets lost by having to unpack and assemble it before each practice. Ideally, your child should be able to grab the instrument, tune it if necessary, and play. There are various types of floor-standing and

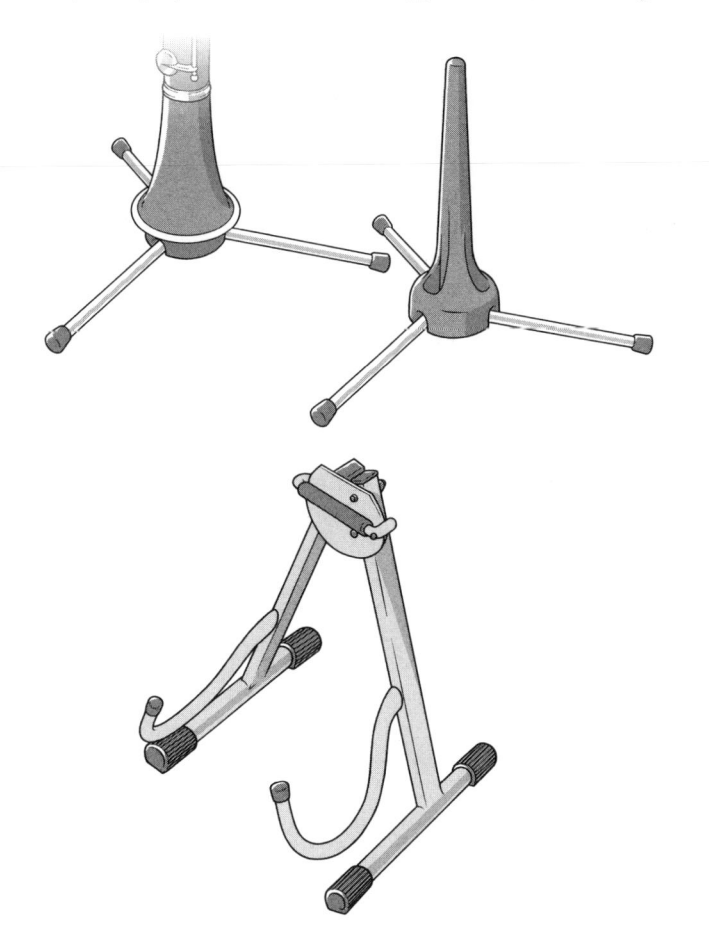

A clarinet stand that easily folds up to a very small size.

Foldable guitar stand.

TIPBOOK MUSIC FOR KIDS AND TEENS

CHAPTER 4

wall-mounted stands and holders for string instruments, wind instruments, and other instruments, so they can sit unpacked and out of the way of people and pets. Special covers can help protect your valuable investments against dust and air-borne dirt.

Music stand

For students who read sheet music, a music stand is a necessity. This very affordable piece of hardware promotes good posture and prevents sore necks, provided it has been set up correctly for your child. Nearly all music stands can be folded into a compact size for transportation, but it's easier if they can be left standing for the next practice session. This also enhances their life expectancy. Is your child required to bring a stand to lessons or rehearsals? Then invest in a second stand and keep that in the instrument case or bag, if possible, so your child can't forget to bring it. A basic music stand will set you back less than twenty dollars.

Two tips

- Most music stands have two 'arms' that **keep the sheet music in place** and prevent music books from flopping closed. As an alternative, you can use a rubber band or clothes pins, or you can have the books spiral-bound so that they stay open.

All kinds of models...

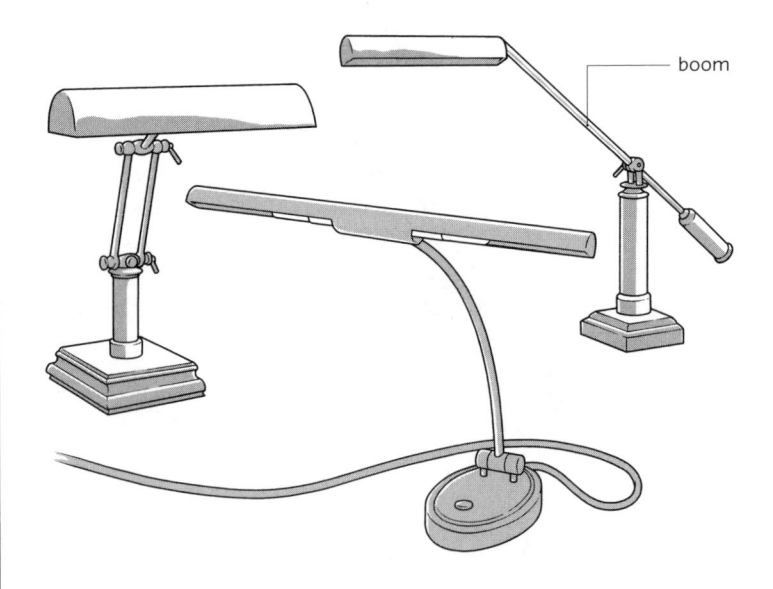

boom

PRACTICING

- Music stands are also available in **bright colors** and heavy-duty orchestra models. The latter are great for home use too, offering additional stability.

Light
Lighting in the room should be sufficient to see the music easily and clearly. An additional small lamp is usually all this takes. Tips:

- There are special, battery powered **lamps** available for music stands. Leds keep power consumption to a minimum.
- Pianos require special **piano lamps**, which are available in a wide variety of models and styles.

Stool or chair
A regular stool or chair will do for students of most instruments. Pianists, keyboard players, drummers, and many other musicians benefit from a special, preferably height-adjustable stool or bench. Without it, posture may be bad and practicing will soon be tiresome.

A drum throne.

Metronome
A metronome is a small mechanical (analog) or electronic (digital) device that ticks or beeps out a steady, adjustable pulse. It's an important practice aid that prevents musicians from speeding up or slowing down the tempo, thus helping to develop one's inner clock. It's also a great device for practicing pieces or difficult bits very slowly (see page 103), and it makes it a lot easier to work on increasing the tempo of pieces and technical exercises step by step.

CHAPTER 4

Like any other tool, metronomes should be used wisely. Don't use a metronome when working on a new piece, for example, or when focusing on a beautiful tone. Also, students who use their metronome too often may become dependent on it. Metronomes are available starting at less than twenty dollars. Many electronic versions can also sound a 440 Hz tuning tone, the standard A to which most instruments are tuned. *Tip:* Software metronomes can be found online (simply search for metronome online), and they're also available as smartphone applications.

Two mechanical metronomes and two electronic ones.

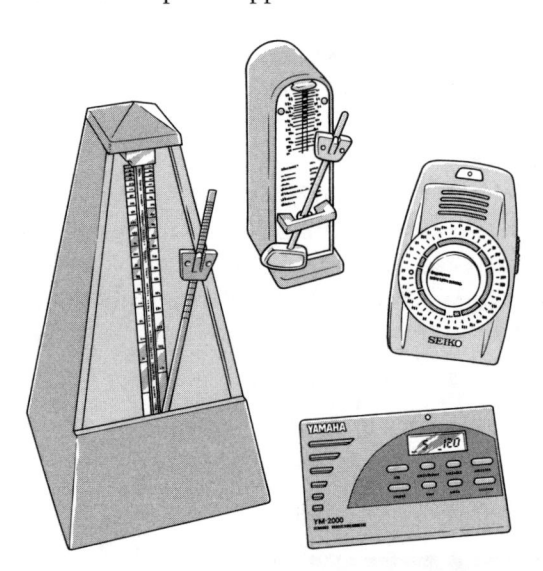

Electronic tuner
Guitar students usually rely on electronic tuners to tune their instrument. The more advanced (chromatic) types of tuners have a display that indicates which note (string) is being played, and whether it is flat (too low; the string needs to be tightened a bit) or sharp (too high; the string should be loosened a bit). Such tuners are known as chromatic tuners. A decent one will set you back some twenty dollars or more. Some models double as a metronome. Online and smartphone tuners (apps) are also available.

Tuning fork
Orchestral string players and other musicians often prefer using a tuning fork. This is a short, two-pronged fork that produces

PRACTICING

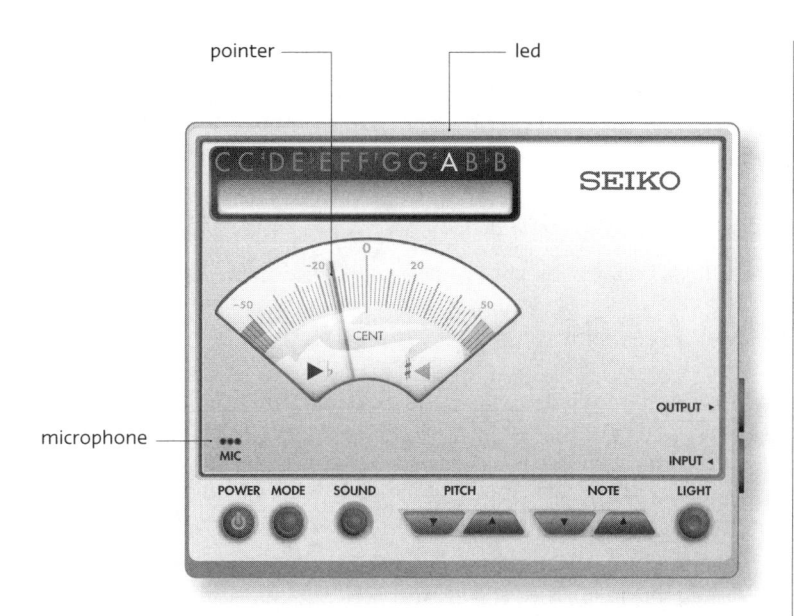

pointer — led

An automatic, chromatic electronic tuner. The A it hears sounds a little flat.

microphone

an A (or another specified pitch) when you tap it on your knee, and gently put the stem against your ear or on the bridge of your instrument.

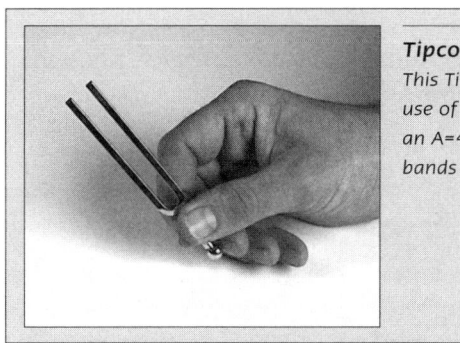

Tipcode KIDS-001
This Tipcodes demonstrates the use of a tuning fork that sounds an A=440, the pitch that most bands and orchestras tune to.

TIPCODE

Sound systems and computers

Having a sound system in the practice area allows your child to play along to prerecorded music, play back a recorded lesson, or maybe even record the practice session. Likewise, a computer can be used to play back CDs, DVDs, and CD-ROMs, to access online lessons and music games, or to record practice sessions (if equipped with the right hardware and software). It's also a helpful tool to compose, arrange, transpose, or create music. Synthesizers, home keyboards, and other digital instruments can be hooked up directly to the computer using MIDI, the musical instrument digital interface that is integrated in all digital music equipment.

AND MORE

There's much more you, your child, and teachers can do to make practice more effective and fun. Here are some additional tips:

- Make sure that you know when your child is extremely busy at school, and consider **lightening up on practice arrangements** that week. You may also ask the teacher to take periods of heavy school workloads into account.
- 'Have you **played the piano** yet?' sounds much more inviting than 'Have you practiced yet?
- Some children love **playing in another room** of the house from time to time, or even outside, if possible.
- Make sure practice time is **uninterrupted**. Ask friends who call to call back, and ask siblings to stay out of the way.
- **Varying a child's assignments** can help to keep things fresh. Some teachers focus on playing a new piece for a month or so, then address sound production or intonation for a couple of weeks, and so on.
- Make sure **the teacher** knows and understands your child. Some children prefer clear, one-way assignments, while others prefer to have a say in things.
- If children tend to forget certain elements of their weekly assignments, or seems to misunderstand the teacher's instructions, ask their teacher to have them **write down their assignment themselves**, in their own words.
- If older kids want to practice at least an hour a day, have them take one or more **short breaks** within that hour.

- Even shorter **micro-breaks** help people of any age stay focused. If you just can't get that one difficult passage down (or handle whatever problem), comb your hair, pet the cat, eat a carrot, or take a sip of water before trying again. Or try again next week!

- The instrument should be in good repair and **tuned properly**. If your child can't tune his or her instrument yet, learn to do it yourself. Ask the teacher for help or consult the relevant Tipbook (see pages 239–243).

- Practicing with **play-along recordings** can be a lot more fun than practicing band or orchestra parts all alone. There are commercially available play-along media, but another option is to record a performance or rehearsal of the band or orchestra your child is in, and have your child play along at home.

- Tell your child to **stop if it hurts**. Playing an instrument should not induce pain. If a certain symptom (from a backache to sore lips) returns every time your child is practicing or playing, consult the teacher. The solution could be as simple as getting a different chair or resetting the music stand.

REDUCING THE SOUND LEVEL

Listening to beginner's practice sessions is usually not very agreeable. Also, practicing seriously sometimes means playing loudly, and on some instruments, learning to play softly takes a lot of time.

Headphones
Instruments that need an amplifier to be heard can be absolutely silent during practice. Simply turn the volume way down, or turn the speaker off completely and plug in a pair of headphones. Most electronic keyboard instruments (digital pianos, keyboards, etc.) have one or two headphone outputs, the second one intended for the teacher, or for a fellow player when performing four-handed pieces. Practice amps for electric guitars and basses usually have a headphone output too. Alternatively, the instrument can be played

CHAPTER 4

over a guitar preamp or bass preamp. This is typically a small unit that features a number of guitar or bass effects, as well as a headphone output. Important: Avoid using headphones at high volume levels to prevent possible hearing damage.

A small affordable amplifier with a headphone output.

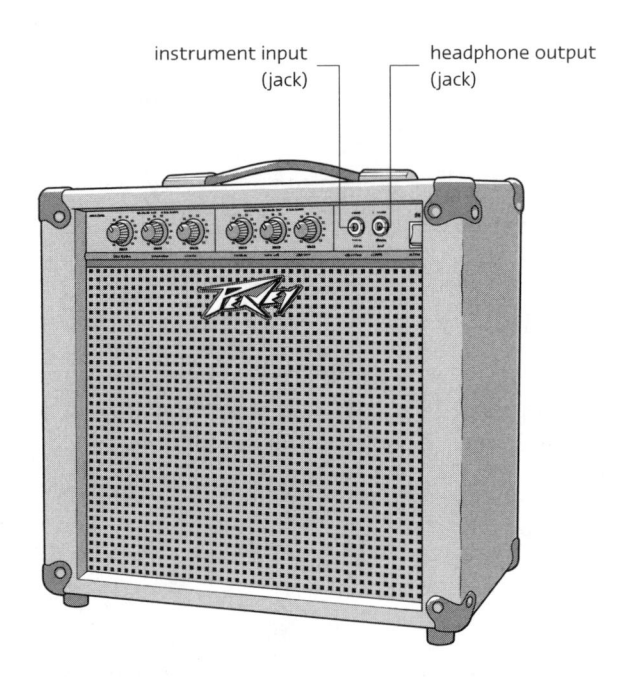

instrument input (jack)

headphone output (jack)

From recorder to drums

Acoustic instruments are instruments that don't need an amplifier to be played: Their sound is amplified 'acoustically'. The lowest sound levels are generated by recorders, violins, and acoustic guitars. The cello and the double bass (a.k.a. upright bass or string bass) sound about as loud, but they also generate contact noise as they rest on the floor when you play them. The sound travels throughout the house and possibly to your neighbors' through floors and walls. The flute, clarinet, oboe, French horn, tuba, and trombone sound a bit louder. The piano produces a sound level similar to these instruments, but it generates quite a bit of contact noise as well. Drums are by far the loudest acoustic instrument. With the bass drum, the bass drum pedal and the hi-hat pedal sitting directly on the floor, drum kits also produce more contact noise than any other instrument.

PRACTICING

Neighbors and housemates
What can you do to keep neighbors and housemates happy if your child chooses to play one of the louder acoustic instruments? One effective solution is to limit practice times to hours when neighbors and housemates won't be bothered, if possible. Communication with all parties is essential in this matter.

The source
The next best solution is to reduce the sound output, which you can do with most, but not all, instruments. The clarinet, the oboe, and the flute are three of the instruments that cannot be effectively muffled.

Brass instruments
For most brass instruments, there are various types of mutes that close off the bell of the instrument. Mutes are removable mufflers or baffles that feature one or more tiny holes that allow very little sound to come though — generally quieting the instrument enough so as not to disturb anyone outside the room you're in. You have to adjust your playing when using a mute, though: You'll need to blow harder, and the mute will raise the pitch slightly, so it's not a good idea to use it routinely. A more expensive option is the Yamaha Silent Brass system. This basically consists of a plastic mute with a built-in microphone, a small amplifier, and a pair of headphones. The amp has an input for a CD or MP3 player, so you can silently play along with prerecorded music. You can also hook up a second Silent Brass, or a home keyboard, for instance. A built-in reverb adds some space and life to the sound.

A practice mute.

Strings
There are two solutions for violinists and cellists.
One is using a practice mute. This short, thick 'comb' slides over the bridge of the instrument where it effectively mutes most of the sound. This implies that it's best not to use one if you're working on your tone. The second solution, which is not usually considered very suitable for beginners, is a Silent Violin or a Silent Cello.

CHAPTER 4

These electric instruments don't have a sound-reinforcing body, but instead feature a small built-in amplifier and a headphone output. An audio input allows your child to hook up an audio player (CD, MP3, etc.) to play along with prerecorded music.

Silent Violin (Yamaha).

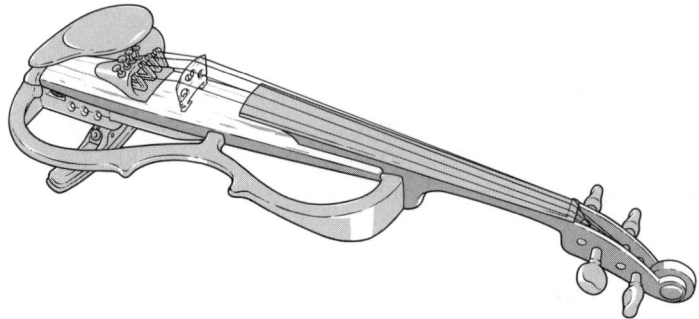

Saxophones
Saxophones can be muted by using a padded ring, or inserting a towel into the bell. This is not very effective, though. These mutes make the lowest notes difficult to play, while higher notes will hardly be dampened at all. After all, most of the tone holes are wide open when you play high notes, so muffling the far end of the instrument has no use. A more effective alternative is a special bag or case that completely covers the instrument, considerably cutting down the volume. The saxophone is played using the three openings of the bag: one for each hand, and one for the mouthpiece. As an alternative, there are electronic wind instruments with a saxophone-style keywork and mouthpiece, but they're quite different from a traditional saxophone.

Piano
Many upright pianos have a muffler pedal or practice pedal. This pedal is located between the other two pedals. Pressing it makes a strip of felt move between the piano's strings and its hammers, muffling the sound to a certain extent. It also changes the feel of the piano, making it a less than ideal solution. As an alternative, many pianos now come with a built-in digital piano. The digital sound, heard through speakers or headphones, is triggered from the keyboard after lowering a so-called hammer-stop rail that prevents the hammers from hitting the strings. Yet another option is to buy a digital piano in addition to or instead of an acoustic

PRACTICING

piano. Though they are still quite different instruments, the gap between them is definitely smaller than it used to be.

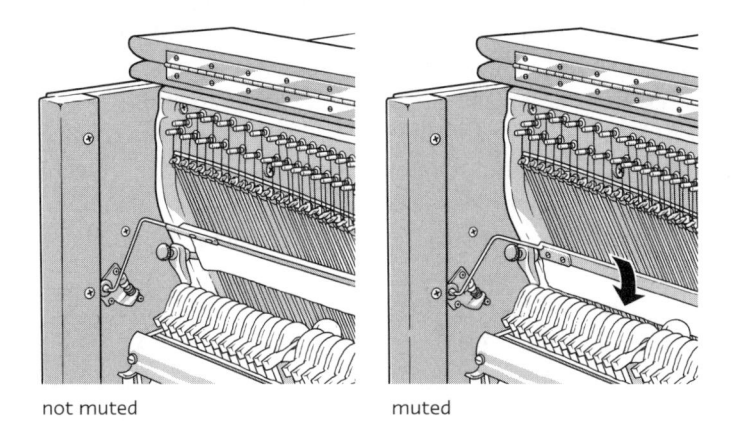

A strip of felt between hammers and strings...

not muted

muted

Drums

There are various solutions for drummers. First, most drum exercises can be played on an almost soundless practice pad. You

An electronic drum set (Roland).

TIPBOOK MUSIC FOR KIDS AND TEENS

can even build an entire drum set using such pads, including the cymbals. Second, acoustic drums can be stuffed with blankets and cushions, or the plastic drum heads can be replaced with soundless mesh heads. The latter solution is more expensive, but yields less sound and a better 'feel.' If the same drum set is used in rehearsals or performances as well, it's better to muffle heads and cymbals with special rubber discs that can easily be removed. A more expensive, yet musically the most satisfying solution is a set of electronic drums, which can be played using headphones. Note that its pedals may still cause some contact noise problems. Electronic drum sets, like most digital pianos and home keyboards, use digital recordings (samples) as a sound source. They can sound and feel close to 'the real thing'.

Someplace else

It's always best to practice an acoustic instrument without mufflers, mutes, or other sound-reducing accessories. So if sound is a problem, consider finding a formal practice space somewhere outside of the house (which is not an option for young kids, of course). Schools and music schools may have practice cubicles that can be used, or there may be practice studios or rehearsal rooms for rent in your vicinity.

Soundproof rooms

It may be possible to soundproof a room in your house. There are books available on sound insulation, you can ask around to find people who sound-proofed a room, or you can hire a specialized contractor to do the job. Alternatively, you can have a prefab soundproof studio installed in your house. Sound-proofing a room may be as costly as a prefab studio, but both solutions can be very effective.

HEARING PROTECTION

Most children's daily practice sessions aren't long enough to cause hearing problems. The drums, again, are an exception to this rule.

PRACTICING

Playing this instrument for fifteen minutes or even less a day could induce irreversible hearing damage, unless the drummer wears some kind of hearing protection.

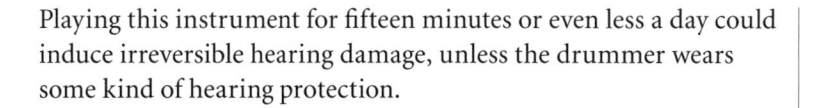

Bands and orchestras

Hearing protection may also be necessary if your child plays in a band or an orchestra. A rehearsing rock band definitely sounds loud enough to more than justify such aids. You may have a hard time convincing your kid to wear some kind of protection, however. Presenting hearing protection as a cool thing will take a lot of effort, but a few (of the many) well-known artists who suffer from hearing loss do endorse such products. Horn sections in bands and orchestras also produce enough sound to cause hearing damage, not only for the players themselves, but for those sitting or walking directly in front of them as well. *Tip:* portable audio players, used with headphones at high volume levels, are a well-known cause for hearing damage, especially among youngsters.

Solutions

Foam earplugs, available at drugstores and hardware stores, are the most affordable form of hearing protection, but they tend to turn music into a muffled, unclear, and unnatural sound. Custom-made ear plugs with replaceable or adjustable filters protect the ears without reducing sound quality. They cost a lot more, but not as much as a pair of hearing aids. Seriously: They are a wise investment, especially for people who play a lot. As an added benefit, these plugs are very effective at loud concerts as well.

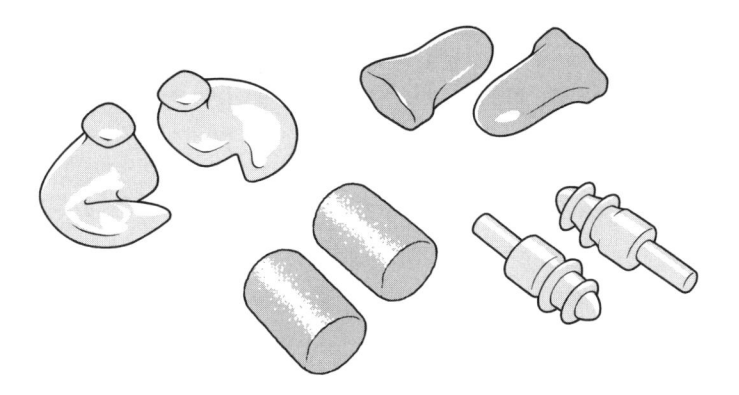

Some affordable types of ear plugs.

In between
In between the low-budget foam plugs and custom-made pugs are various other types of hearing protection, with or without special filters. They're available from most music stores and usually come in a variety of standard sizes.

THE INGREDIENTS
A well-structured practice routine is one of the main keys to effective practice. Depending on the student's level of playing, the main ingredients of a practice session are:

- Warming up
- Scales and broken chords
- Etudes
- Sight-reading
- New pieces
- Review

For beginning students, the list is shorter, with elements being added as they progress.

Tuning
Most instruments need to be tuned, or the tuning needs to be checked before playing. This is where the practice session really begins. As said before, it is easiest if the instrument is always ready to be played — unpacked and assembled. You may want to have valuable and vulnerable instruments packed when they're not being played, however. Also, replaceable parts such as strings, and the leather pads on woodwind instruments, tend to last longer if the instrument is covered in between practice sessions.

Warming up
Playing music requires a warm up, just like sports do. Advanced and professional musicians can even get injured from playing demanding pieces without a decent warm up. For beginners and

intermediate players, the first few minutes of playing are basically meant to get into mood for playing, to get the fingers going, and to get 'into the instrument.' It even helps if you take a good long look at your instrument before you play your first notes. Warm-up exercises are not technically demanding. They're the ideal setting for focusing on tone quality, because they allow students to really listen to the sound tone they're producing.

Scales, broken chords, and etudes

Scales and broken chords are often used for warm ups, but they're also practiced separately as exercises that increase playing proficiency, allowing the fingers to do what the mind tells them to. Etudes are pieces written with that same goal in mind.

Tipcode KIDS-002
This Tipcode plays some very basic scales, chords, and broken chords.

More fun

Many kids dislike playing scales, etudes, and similar exercise material. It's not as much fun as playing 'real' pieces, and the exercises often seem meaningless. A good teacher might be able to make children understand why they're so essential, inspiring their students to play them with all their heart. Besides, there are various ways to make playing these exercises more fun. Here are some ideas to pass along to your child:

- Focusing on **your tone** really helps; imagine what a scale would sound like when played by your all-time favorite musician!
- Playing scales as if they were **beautiful pieces of music** makes a difference too.

CHAPTER 4

- Make the **volume go up** as you play the scale upwards, and vice versa.
- **Speed up** when playing upwards, and vice versa.
- Speed up and **get loude**r one way, and vice versa.
- Play scales in **the rhythm of a song** you like, or play them as triplets.
- Pianists: Play F-major with your **left hand** and C-major with your **right hand**, and experiment with other pairs of scales.

New pieces
Adding new pieces is necessary to keep students progressing, to keep them challenged, to expand their repertoire, and to raise their general level of playing. Check pages 103–105 for tips on handling new pieces.

Reviewing repertoire
When students play pieces they already know, there's no struggle, so they're simply playing music. It's as close to performing as practicing will get — and that's what playing is all about, for most students. Reviewing older pieces also keeps their repertoire alive.

Sight-reading
Sight-reading is an essential part of various exams and competitions. It is much the same as reading a story or an article to someone, be it that playing while reading the music is quite a bit harder than reading a book out loud. Sight-reading is an important skill for all musicians who want or need to play in situations where they will be expected to perform or rehearse without prior preparation (such as working in recording studios).

And more
A practicing session can consist of lots of other ingredients, such as:

- **Specific exercises** (dynamics, phrasing, bowing, improvisation, ear training, extending your range with higher or lower notes, etc.).
- **Experimenting**: Explore the instrument, try to discover new sounds or playing techniques, try to figure out a melody you've heard, think up new melodies, etc.

- **Play along** with prerecorded music. Numerous self-taught players learned their instrument this way, and it's a valid, fun, and effective technique for all musicians that don't have a band or an orchestra at their disposal.

Recitals

A short recital, in which your kid plays a new piece or an older song for you, can make a great practice session finale. Children will get the opportunity to perform, and you'll hear how they've progressed. Also, playing 'in public' on a regular basis can help diminish performance anxiety and teach them to continue playing through mistakes. Generally, when the teacher is the first to hear a new song, most children make mistakes they didn't make when they played it at home (see page 78), so short recitals help prepare them for playing for their teacher as well. A recital once a week will usually do, but some children may want you to come listen every day.

> ### Family and friends
> Note that children who love to perform for you may not want to do so for other family members or friends, and the ones who like to play for you now may say 'no' as they get into their teens and become more self-conscious. Forcing children to perform is probably the best way to make them want to quit entirely.

TIP

Maintenance

Depending on the instrument, a couple of minutes at the end of each practice session should be dedicated to daily instrument maintenance. Wind instruments have to be disassembled and dried, orchestral string players will need to take care of their bow, guitar and bass guitar strings need to be cleaned, and so on. Specific instructions for most popular instruments can be found in the Tipbooks listed on pages 239–243.

CHAPTER 4

STRUCTURE

One of your main roles, depending on your child's age and degree of independence, will be to help structure their practice sessions. You can't expect young children to effectively plan fifteen minutes or half an hour of activities.

Time management
Make sure that the practice sessions are given a permanent slot in their daily routine, along with school, homework, seeing friends, sports, watching TV or gaming, chatting, and other activities. Time management needs to be taught.

The beginning
It's usually best to start a practice session with something that's relatively easy to play, such as scales, or a familiar piece of music, just to get things going. Doing the hard stuff first may be an effective way to handle homework, but when it comes to music, starting off with a new piece, tricky sections, or demanding exercises can be quite frustrating.

The end and in between
Ending the session with a review of their older repertoire is like rewarding students for having practiced. They get to play something they know and that they've worked on before. In between, the choice is basically up to the student or you, while their teacher may have helpful suggestions based on the child's learning style or way of practicing. A tip: Some students prefer the safety of doing things in the same order every time, while others dislike such routines.

Two or three sessions
If practice time is divided into two or more sessions, it'll probably be most effective to do a little of everything in each session rather than spending the first session only on scales, the second on a new piece, the third on older repertoire, etc. — but some children may just prefer the latter.

PRACTICING

Clock?
Some experts advise you to dedicate a certain amount of time to each element of a practice session: a five minute warm-up, ten minutes on etudes, ten on the new piece, and another five to play something familiar. Others will tell you to get rid of the clock, as you want children to focus on what they're playing rather than on the minutes passing by. But without a clock present, you should probably see to it that your child doesn't spend half an hour playing scales (right!), so there's no time left for the other assignments. If the assignments have been structured well and the teacher has provided your child with checkpoints, this will probably not happen. Still, it's good to keep an eye on things. You may even want to listen in and jot down how much time your child spends on warming up, on scales, and so on, for feedback purposes.

Goals
For older children, it can be helpful to talk about the goals they've set for each practice session, apart from those set by their teacher. When they're old enough, they can start setting their own goals.

Short, medium, long
The clearer one's goals are, the easier it will be to practice effectively. When defining goals, it often helps to distinguish:

- **long-term goals** (I'd like to join such-and-such band, or play a solo recital by the end of the year, or become a professional musician);

- **mid-term goals** (I'd like to finish this book, or be able to play these pieces);

- and **short-term goals**, which may differ for each practice session (I'd like to memorize this piece, or play that section ten times without a mistake).

CHAPTER 4

PRACTICING TECHNIQUES

Practicing efficiently is also a matter of applying the right practicing techniques. Improving your tone requires a different technique than increasing your speed, or tackling a new piece.

Small jobs
One of the best ways to make practice session more effective and fun is to break down large jobs into a number of small jobs. Rather than tackling a new piece from beginning to end, break it down into four or eight measures to be played per day, for example. This way, the student can have a small success every day, rather than fighting to master the entire piece in one week.

Revision
If a new piece is broken up into sections comprised of a number of bars, reviewing the sections that were done on previous days should be an essential part of each practice session. Learning an instrument is most effectively done through frequent repetition. (In various languages, the word for 'practice' literally means repetition!)

The right notes
Repetition results in long-term memory storage, which is good. The problem, however, is that your memory does not select what should be stored and what should not: If you consistently repeat an incorrect passage, that's what will be stored. If you play the wrong note half of the time, there's a fifty-fifty chance that the wrong note will come out at your performance. So when students repeat things, they have to make that they play the right notes.

Five or ten
Some teachers may advise students to move to the next section only when they're able to play the current section correctly five (or ten) times in a row. If they make a mistake, they have to start counting all over again until they get all five (or ten) correct. Other teachers may not be concerned with the number of repetitions, as long as students play it right the final time. That

way, the player's fingers are supposed to 'remember' the right moves.

Slow down

A difficult passage may be hard to play correctly, and playing it right five times in a row may seem impossible. The solution is to slow things down. Slow, in this case, means really slow. Take one, two, or more seconds for every note, and disregard note values for now. Take a metronome, set it at 60 BPM (i.e., 60 beats per minute, equaling one beat per second), and let it tick two or three times before moving on to the next note. Such slow tempos make students aware of the movements their fingers have to make to get from note to note, or from chord to chord.

> **Tone**
> For advanced players, practicing a piece really slowly is also a good way to work on their tone, and to get the smallest nuances of a piece right: dynamics, intonation, phrasing, and everything else beyond hitting the right notes at the right time.

A NEW PIECE

There are also various practicing techniques for handling new pieces. As mentioned before, a piece can be divided up into four bar, eight bar, or longer sections, revising the previous sections (and playing them absolutely correctly) before moving on to the next section. This is just one of many approaches, and all of these approaches can be mixed to come up with a combination that works well for your child.

Challenge

Starting a new piece is a positive challenge for some children, while it makes others feel as if they have to start all over again.

CHAPTER 4

A good teacher takes that into account, and any student will eventually understand that avoiding new pieces will yield no progress. Also, learning to tackle new pieces helps students to tackle other problems and to deal with new, complex subjects as well. This is actually one of the reasons that music students tend to perform better in various other academic fields. Some of the tips below apply to more advanced students only; others work for beginners too.

Listen
As said before, it is essential that students practice a piece playing only the correct notes. It helps if they can first listen to the music so they know what it's supposed to sound like before attempting to play it. The teacher can play a new piece for them, or they can listen to a recorded version.

Read along
Reading along while listening to a new piece helps students relate the notes to the music. With complex pieces, it can be helpful to study the part visually before listening to it, so repeats and other markings don't come as a surprise when reading along with the music. Reading the music in advance also provides the opportunity to check out all dynamic signs and tempo markings, to locate accidentals (flats, sharps, naturals), and numerous other details and characteristics of the piece — without worrying about playing the right notes at that same time.

More
It's also helpful if teachers tell their students about the music they're going to play: the general character of the piece, its form (12-bar blues or 32-bar AABA? Rondo or suite?), the style, the composer, the era in which it was written, and so on. After all, there's more to music than playing the notes in the correct order.

Step by step
Beginning players are often advised to approach a new piece step by step. First, clap the rhythm of the notes, counting aloud as you go. When you've got the rhythm down, play the melody without paying attention to the rhythm. Once you can clap the rhythm and

play the right notes, combine the two — very, very slowly. This approach works well for advanced players too. Pianists and other keyboard players can practice the left hand part first, followed by the right hand, before attempting to play a new piece with both hands.

The trouble spots
Alternatively, depending on their ability and the complexity of the piece, students can play the piece at a very easy tempo, spotting the difficult bits as they go. Playing a piece this way, with mistakes and all, provides a general idea of what it is about (assuming you haven't heard it before). Other players rather start by locating the tricky bits and figure them out first. A tip: when working on a tricky section, always include a few notes or bars before and after that particular section in order to make the tricky section a part of the whole thing, rather than an isolated hurdle that might scare you off every time you see it coming.

Analyzing the trouble spots
If children have a problem with a certain section, they can simply play it again and again (and again) until they get it right; but it might be more effective to find out what's causing the problem in the first place. Is it the fingering (which fingers to use for which note)? The rhythm? Or is it hard to play the part with the left hand while the right hand is doing something else? Or is it a note that's too high or too low for their current range?

Your help
Children may welcome your help in analyzing what the problem is. After all, you are the one who's around when they get stuck; not their teacher. You don't need to play an instrument to help your kid identify the problem. All it takes is asking the right questions so they can figure it out on their own.

Tackle
One step beyond analyzing the trouble spots is developing exercises that help the student tackle them. This is something advanced players do for themselves, and something that teachers should teach their students.

CHAPTER 4

MEMORIZING

Opinions differ as to whether students should memorize music. Some teachers insist that they should; others feel that memorizing music should be optional, unless a student is considering a professional career in music.

Why?
Why would a teacher require that your child memorizes a piece that can be simply read from sheet music? Here's what they might tell their students:

- It makes you a **better musician**. If you're not concentrating on which notes to play, you can fully focus on other elements — tone, phrasing, dynamics, and so on — and listen to yourself play. Also, to play from memory you have to *really* know a piece inside out, which can only help improve your performance.

- Guitarists, pianists (and other keyboard players), and harpists who play by heart can watch their hands as they play, which may be very helpful if they have to make big leaps. Not a very professional approach, but **it can be handy**.

- It **makes you look good**. Professional soloists play without sheet music, so why can't you?

Why not?
And what do the other teachers say?

- Of course, there's no need to keep students from memorizing music (and some are extremely good at it), but **why force them**?

- Being required to play without sheet music makes a performance an **even more stressful** event — and wasn't making music about enjoying yourself?

- Worrying about what'll happen if you forget the piece does not inspire a good performance. It takes away more energy from the music than reading notes does. In other words, some just need sheet music to play well, even while others might **play better without it**.

PRACTICING

- For students who are not good at memorizing, learning pieces by heart will take up valuable time that's probably better spent on things they *can* **do to improve and to grow musically**.

- Forcing students to do things they don't like or are not good at can even make them want to quit (and of course, teachers and parents should be aware that in some cases, this is just **typical reluctance** that needs to be overcome).

Marching
Members of marching bands' drum lines are typically required to memorize their parts, and the same usually goes for musicians in other bands where a choreography or drill is an essential part of the performance. After all, it is hard to play, move, and read at the same time. Some directors encourage their band members to play by heart, but don't force them to. A so-called 'flip folder' or a basic lyre that holds the score can be attached to any marching instrument.

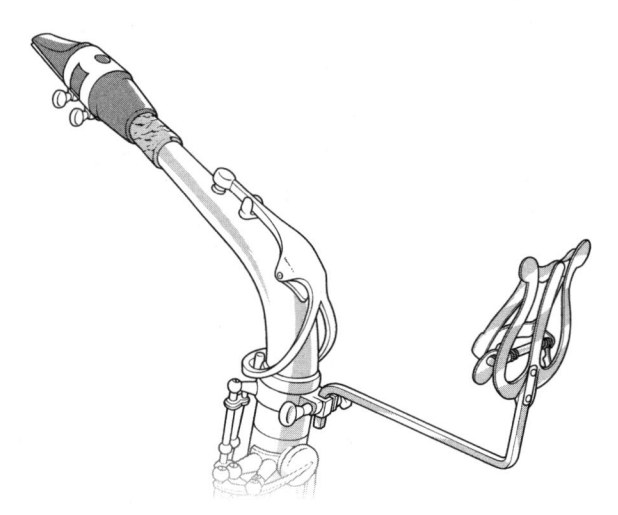

A basic lyre.

Techniques and tips
There are various ways and techniques to memorize music. What the best way is depends on the student, the level of playing, and other factors. The following shortlist offers some suggestions that you can discuss with your child. The same list will help you recognize how your child handles things.

CHAPTER 4

- Students can memorize a piece **as they learn it**, or they can wait to memorize it until they can play it correctly.

- Memorize **small sections** at a time. For some students, a small section is one or two bars; for others, it's half a page. Start with the first section, and add subsequent sections only after the previous sections have been mastered.

- Some students memorize **the difficult parts** first, repeating them so often that they become as easy to play as the rest of the piece. Only after mastering the difficult parts do they include the other sections. *Tip:* Many teachers claim that you should never play a piece in any other order than the one intended.

- Most musicians memorize a piece from beginning to the end, but there are those who prefer to do it the other way around, working their way back to the beginning.

- Suggest students to memorize **bits and pieces** as they go. They should try not to look at the music while they're playing, glancing up only as they feel they need to. Bit by bit, over time, they will learn to play the entire piece by heart.

- If students repeat a piece or a section over and over, they're using their **finger memory** or tactile memory. The fingers then know what to do because they've been trained to execute the patterns that are required for that piece of music. It's a relatively easy way to memorize music, but it's not very reliable. Changing the tempo of the piece may confuse the player (or his fingers). The best way to find out if a piece of music has been properly memorized is to play it at an extremely slow tempo and see what happens.

- Another approach is to **analyze the piece** step by step, studying every single aspect of it. This requires a lot of knowledge (scales, harmony, etc.), but it's the most reliable way to memorize a composition.

- Practicing a piece **away from the instrument** may help memorizing it. Suggest children to play it in their imagination, first with, then without the score in front of them. This is referred to as shadow practicing or armchair memorizing. Students can also try to hear the piece in their heads without

PRACTICING

playing it, before they go to sleep, or on their way to school, or they can sing it while taking a shower.

- It also helps to make up a story that fits the music!
- **Slow practicing** is good for memorizing music.
- And when you're almost done, **put the book away**. Don't leave it on the music stand, pretending or trying not to peek; put it in the other room. Out of sight, out of mind? Then try again.

5

Guidance and Motivation

Your guidance and support is essential to your child's music education. As you see your child every day, you will probably be able to spot a growing lack of interest in music much sooner than a teacher will. What can you do to guide children and reduce the chance of them quitting?

CHAPTER 5

First of all, it is important that you take your child's musical endeavors seriously. Show your interest by asking them about their lessons, their teacher, their assignments, the pieces they play, the band director, their fellow band members, and so on. Try asking them questions that invite them to contemplate. Open questions like 'What do you like best about your teacher?' or 'What was it that you didn't like about that piece you had to play?' are more effective than questions that can be answered with a simple yes or no. Make this a recurring topic at the dinner table, while taking them to school, or use any other opportunity for a brief dialog. Also ask them about their assignments for the coming week, or ask them to play for you after their weekly lesson, so you know what they're up to, and so they know that you know.

Yell?
Children are usually not yelled at because they didn't watch TV, play with friends, or have fun. So should they be yelled at for not having practiced? That would make practicing too much like the other things most children would rather not do, from washing dishes to cleaning up the mess they made. It may be wiser to commend them for the little practice they *did* do. And when you hear them play, tell them what you liked or what you thought was really good, rather than hassling them about the mistakes they made.

Imposing a discipline
That doesn't mean you can't instill a sense of discipline. Many musicians, professional and amateur, are actually grateful that their parents made them practice. (And they still remember the trouble that caused, but 'You chose to play this instrument, so…') Whether you want to go this route may depend on whether you see your child's musical activities as a mere hobby, or as an essential part of their education.

Positive feedback
Whichever way you handle this, positive feedback is always crucial if you want your child to keep on playing. Discussing your children's progress with their teacher in their presence can make them really proud. Also try to keep track of their progress, and give them feedback: 'This piece sounds a lot better now' or 'Wasn't that

the song you could not play two weeks ago? Great!' This is more effective than saying, 'You did well today.' The more specific you are, the more welcome and appreciated the compliment will be.

> **Back off**
> Being asked, 'Have you practiced?' every day can make your child want to stop completely. Backing off may help. Children may even start practicing as soon as you stop nagging them. If you've noticed their enthusiasm at lessons and/or practice sessions has faded, perhaps backing off from attending these activities will help.

Co-teach?
Certain music programs require that parents be very actively involved in their children's education; they are expected to be their children's home teacher. If your child is taking private lessons, however, you will usually not be expected to co-teach. In these situations, your genuine interest is most welcome, but you are encouraged not to interfere with your children's assignments or advise them to do things differently than what their teacher has told them. Your child will probably be confused if you do.

Different books
Likewise, if you plan to buy songbooks or method books other than those specified by the music teacher, call the teacher for suggestions or get their approval of a desired book before you spend your money. You are free to purchase whatever you want, of course, but getting the wrong books can conflict with the teacher's methodology, and your child will end up suffering as a result. If children show a strong dislike toward the pieces their teacher is having them play, then listen to their arguments and talk to the teacher, rather than just substituting the teacher's selections with something the child wants but the teacher hasn't approved.

Get to know the instrument
Another way to become involved is to take a few lessons on the

CHAPTER 5

instrument yourself. This will help you understand what your child is going through. You may even like it so much that you'll end up playing duets together! Also, children often appreciate your 'technical' assistance in the maintenance of their instrument, from changing strings to replacing and tuning drum heads.

Great motivator

Does your child have anyone to play with? Being in a band or an orchestra is one of the greatest motivators, and the opportunity to play duets with a neighbor or friend can have the same inspiring effect. There's more on the benefits of playing in an ensemble in Chapter 8, which also covers the various types of bands, orchestras, and other groups.

Rewards

Positive feedback is a great motivator, and so is success. Children also love rewards. As a parent, you know what inspires your child. Being allowed to pick what's for dinner, a trip to the movies, or any other activity they like can be the perfect rewards for their musical efforts. There are lots of music-related gifts, too: new strings for their guitar (having them replaced before they break is not a real luxury, but it sure can feel that way), a new drum head (same here), a nice reed holder, other accessories, a CD of their favorite artist, a concert ticket, and so on. You can turn one 'large' reward into a number of small, very affordable ones. Simply give them one or more colorful stickers for every single goal they achieve (mastering a scale or a new piece, finishing a book...) and promise them a CD of their choice when they have collected twenty stickers, for example.

Awards

Children love tangible proof of their achievements, so many teachers have different ways of rewarding their students, such as a sticker or an ink stamp for every completed assignment. Others use different types of awards (e.g., one for every book a student completes) and certificates (e.g., for every year or two years of study). *Tip*: Frame these precious papers for your child! Another tip: Take photos of your child practicing or when they're performing, either at home, or at a competition or a studio recital.

GUIDANCE AND MOTIVATION

These photos, plus things like the program from an event, can be collected and saved in a musical scrapbook for your child.

Contract
Another approach to keeping children motivated to play is to have them sign a contract of their musical aspirations, promising in writing that they will stick with the chosen instrument for one or even two years, and that they'll complete their musical assignments every week. While many educators and parents strongly believe this works, you may wonder if you yourself would be willing to sign such a contract when you begin a new hobby. And do children have to sign contracts for other things they really *like* doing? Still, it may be a viable approach for kids who quit any new activity within a couple of weeks, or for children who feel that a contract proves that their plans are being taken really seriously. It goes without saying that really young children will not be able to grasp the concept of a contract.

Their own money
You could also consider having your child invest some of their own money into their instrument. Even if it's a dollar a month, this investment can make them aware of the value of the instrument, and it may keep them from quitting too easily.

> **Off days**
> Everyone has off days, and so do children. Forcing a child to play when he or she is really not in the mood may not be a good idea. The likelihood that any progress would be made in such cases is close to nil, and if music becomes an obligation, the fun may soon be gone. Still, it can't hurt to suggest that they play just one of their favorite songs that day — but if that doesn't work, let go.

More off days
If your child doesn't feel like playing more than once a week, or for a longer period of time, it's time to find out what's going on.

CHAPTER 5

Children will often say that they 'just don't feel like it.' Telling them to 'feel like it' or be motivated won't really help either. You need to find out why they feel the way they do. The sooner you get to the bottom of their lack of interest, the more likely it is that you can turn things around and get them playing again. Some random thoughts:

- It might be that they **don't like the music** they play anymore. Musical preferences change over time.

- The same can go for **their teacher**. Someone could be your son's favorite teacher one day, then not the next. He may need someone new to inspire him.

- Some children want to quit because they're being harassed by fellow band members, or because the band director makes them feel **insecure** about their musical capabilities. These kinds of situations are difficult for children to reveal, so something of this nature could be behind their 'just not feeling like it anymore.'

- Also, the **level of musicianship** of the ensemble they're in may be too high (making them afraid to fail) or too low (leaving them bored and uninspired).

- Your child may have serious **problems in reading music**, keeping him or her from progressing as fast as they otherwise could. A stronger focus on playing by ear and improvising may help.

- Musicians of all levels experience recurrent periods in which they **don't seem to progress**, as described on page 22. Telling your child that even professionals — and their favorite artists — go through such times may help. It is like hitting a plateau on your way up the mountain; you just walk while nothing happens. And then, all of a sudden, you find your way to the next plateau, with numerous new things to discover.

- **Shifting focus** is a technique that may help in periods of slow or no progress. If mastering new pieces seems to be the problem, it can be good to focus on tone production or technique for a while, or vice versa. A change of activities can help to keep things fresh and rewarding. Talk to your child's teacher!

GUIDANCE AND MOTIVATION

- **Time management** may be a problem. If your child feels that practice sessions have to be squeezed in with loads of other activities, practicing will hardly ever be fun — it's just another thing that needs to be done. Help your child by scheduling things differently.

- If **schoolwork** demands most of their time because of special projects or exams, or in times of emotional stress, children may be grateful if you just let them play and enjoy their music, rather than expecting noticeable progress. Make sure their teacher knows, and do help them get back to their regular practice routine when things are back to normal.

- Make sure your child feels **free to speak up** when their music assignments are more than they can handle (or less than what they need to keep them motivated!).

- There's no use practicing what you're good at, but the joy of making music will soon fade if children focus solely on what they're not so good at. If playing faster tempos is a problem, focusing too much on speed may be extremely frustrating. So why not have them **play things they like**? If that makes them play more, their agility on the instrument will increase automatically.

- Do they still like **the instrument** they're playing? Chances are they might not if they were assigned an instrument rather than being allowed to choose their favorite. Regardless, a growing dislike of their current instrument will make them want to quit. As they may not be able to articulate this, you may hear, 'I don't feel like it anymore' instead.

- Is their instrument in **good repair**? Does it make playing fun and easy? Does it allow them to grow musically? (See page 120.)

- Does your child have any **musician friends**? If all of their friends are playing ball, it may be hard to focus on scales and etudes.

- And if children really want to quit, you should **perhaps just let them**. Be happy that you have tried to instill a love of music in your child, but realize that you can't force someone to love playing. Maybe they'll pick up an instrument again later in life.

CHAPTER 5

Danger zones

Kids could decide they want to stop playing anytime, but there are specific 'danger zones' to watch out for. The first is in or around the second half of the first year of lessons, as progress often slows and the excitement has worn off. The second is around age twelve, when a lot of changes are taking place, as discussed on page 15. Simply paying a little extra attention to your children may be enough to keep them playing!

6

Borrowing, Renting, or Buying?

Your child wants to play an instrument, so you need to get one. Is it wise to borrow one from a friend? Does your child's school provide instruments, or should you rent, lease, or buy one? And if you do decide to rent or buy an instrument, where do you go? This chapter sheds some light on these topics, and provides basic information on the costs of playing an instrument, from maintenance and sheet music to band and exam fees.

CHAPTER 6

If you want your children to enjoy playing, and if you'd prefer them to do so for many years, a good instrument is vital. Numerous children have quit because they had to practice on an out-of-tune piano with keys that stuck, or a leaky flute. For wind instruments, choosing the right mouthpiece for your child is essential. Reed players need good reeds. And so on… Children cannot understand the limitations of a faulty instrument and will likely blame themselves when they fail to progress or play well. And once, however wrongfully, they're convinced they cannot play, they will probably quit.

School and family instruments
Unfortunately, the instruments that you may borrow or rent from your child's school are not always in a decent state of repair. When in doubt, have the instrument assessed by the technician at your local music store, a musician who specializes in that instrument, or a teacher.

Value for money
The quality of new musical instruments has generally gone up while prices have gone down, so you typically get a lot of value for your money. A decent electric or acoustic guitar can be purchased for less than one hundred and fifty dollars, for example. Wind instruments tend to be more critical. The most affordable flutes, clarinets, or saxophones may be hard if not impossible to adjust or repair, keys may go out of adjustment more easily, bending or soldering them may damage the instrument, and spare parts may not be available.

> ### Teachers
> Many teachers will simply refuse to teach a child who brings an unplayable instrument to lessons. Of course, teachers will typically offer advice on renting or buying a proper instrument beforehand. Note that teachers at institutions may be not allowed to suggest where to buy or rent an instrument!

Workable option
Not all experts dislike such instruments, however. Some consider them workable enough options for children who are known to change their minds on what they want to eat halfway through lunch, and who may act likewise when it comes to the instrument they want to play. Besides, the fact that the instrument is their own, rather than rented, may be an extra motivator.

The best you can get
Most instruments come in a wide range of prices. More expensive instruments usually offer a better sound, they have a longer life expectancy, they feature higher quality materials and craftsmanship, they have a higher resale value, and they're usually easier to play than inexpensive models. Still, while it's usually wise to buy the best instrument you can afford, it's probably not a good idea to buy your eight-year-old a six-thousand dollar saxophone.

Pro?
Many companies distinguish three quality categories for most musical instruments: beginner or student-line models, intermediate or step-up instruments, and professional instruments. There are three problems with such categorizations.

- The first problem is that they tell you virtually nothing about **the actual cost** of the instruments. For example, a 'student-line' bassoon costs a whole lot more than an 'intermediate' guitar.

- The second problem is that **opinions differ** as to the price ranges per category: What some call a step-up flute, is a beginner's instrument to others.

- The third problem is that the term 'professional' is the **most misused word** in the music industry. Many instruments with a 'pro' label are really made and priced for beginners. True professional instruments don't need such labels. Please refer to the various instrument Tipbooks for more information (see pages 239–243).

How much?
If you plan to buy your child an instrument, most teachers will advise you not to purchase the least expensive one you can

CHAPTER 6

find, but to instead go for a decent, dependable instrument that your budding musician will enjoy for at least a couple of years. What do such 'decent' instruments cost, and how much is a truly inexpensive one? A tip in advance: Many schools own the more expensive types of instruments and provide them to their students.

- A decent **recorder** would be one of the least expensive choices of instruments at around fifty dollars. You can get a plastic one for less than ten.

- Think two hundred dollars for an **acoustic guitar**, and even less for an **electric** one. The latter isn't complete, however, without another hundred or two for a practice amp, strap, and picks.

- Decent **home keyboards** start at around three hundred dollars. A good digital piano with a hammer action keyboard (see page 201) can cost three times as much.

- New **acoustic pianos** start around fifteen hundred dollars, but you're often better off with one that's at least twice that price.

A French horn.

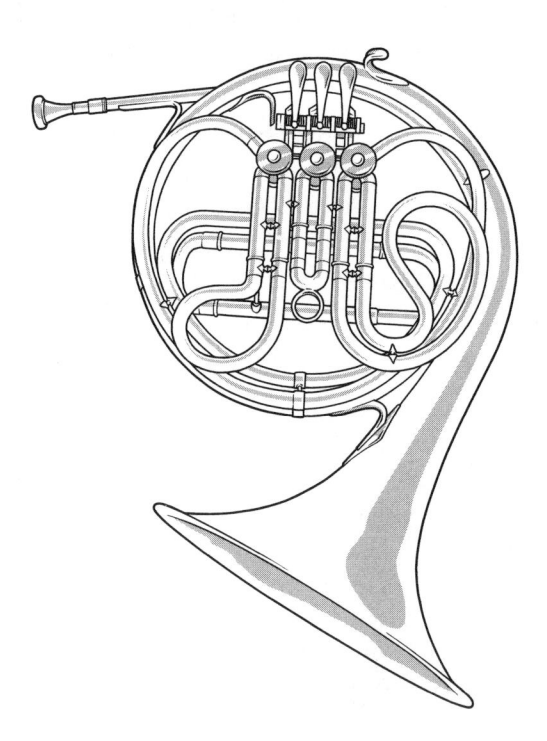

BORROWING, RENTING, OR BUYING?

- Most decent **woodwind instruments** will set you back some five hundred dollars or more. Some are more expensive: bassoons easily cost three thousand dollars.

- Expect to pay between three and four hundred dollars for a decent trumpet or other small **brasswinds**, such as a cornet. French horns are more expensive; student models soon cost seven or eight hundred dollars, and tubas start around two thousand dollars.

- Few people buy their child a **violin** before they're ready for a full-sized instrument, at around the age of twelve or later. Decent, complete outfits (violin, bow, case) are typically around seven or eight hundred dollars (but you can find them as low as a hundred). Cello outfits cost more, and so do double basses.

- Step-up and professional **drum sets** are usually sold without cymbals. Expect to pay between one thousand and fifteen hundred dollars for a complete set (five drums, one or two cymbals, and a pair of hi-hat cymbals). Such a set-up will be good enough for performance purposes; you can find sets for less than three hundred as well.

Less and more

As the quality of low-priced instruments continues to increase, you may be able to buy a decent beginner's instrument for very little money. However, follow experts' advice to prevent disappointments. To the layman's eye, a forty dollar guitar may look exactly like a six-hundred dollar one, but the less expensive one may need to be retuned every five minutes, for example, or it may sound terribly out of tune as it is played beyond the first few positions.

The sky is the limit

If you really have money to spend, the sky is the limit. You can easily spend a thousand dollars on a single cymbal, a handmade flute may cost fifty thousand or more (but it's hard to find a saxophone or a clarinet that costs more than ten!), a professional harp can cost thirty thousand, some grand pianos sell for two hundred thousand dollars, and millions have been paid for Stradivarius violins or Guarnerius cellos.

CHAPTER 6

Grand pianos cost anywhere between some five thousand and two hundred thousand dollars or more.

BORROWING

The opportunity to borrow an instrument may be very tempting, but the instruments at hand are often not the best ones. This goes especially for so-called 'family' instruments. Many types of wind instruments will be unplayable if they haven't been used and maintained for a couple of years or more, and the same goes for pianos. A technician will be able to tell you how much it will cost to get the instrument back into playing condition again. With guitars, your chances are better that time will not have degraded their quality, and there are millions of guitars in attics eagerly waiting to be played again. Small children need a smaller-sized guitar, though, as discussed on page 158. If you borrow an instrument, you may want to get the terms of your lending agreement in writing (e.g., what to do if the instrument gets damaged or lost).

Please don't
Some schools have instruments for all of their first-year band members, and they may specifically ask you *not* to buy your child an instrument. Having the students play a school-owned instrument allows for instrument changes throughout the first year, initiated either by the school or your child. Has your child had a favorite instrument since long before being able to join the school program? Then you may of course consider purchasing an instrument and finding your youngster a private teacher.

RENTING OR LEASING

Some schools and many music stores have rental instruments available on lease plans. Schools usually charge very low (often nominal) fees.

Return or sell
Renting or leasing an instrument from a music store will be more expensive in the long run than buying one. The main advantage of renting or leasing is that you can simply return the instrument if your child decides to quit. If you have purchased an instrument, you'll have to resell it, which isn't always easy to do. *Tip:* Some rental and lease plans allow your child to switch to another instrument.

Maintenance and insurance
Maintenance is usually included in the rental fee, but some plans offer it as a separate expense. The main thing is to make sure you don't have to worry about it. Insurance may be included as well. Make sure you understand what is and isn't covered under your lease or rental plan.

Fractional instruments
For violins and the other orchestral string instruments that come in fractional sizes, renting had another advantage: Children will need larger-sized instruments as they grow. Most of these plans provide children with a size-up as soon as necessary. You should

CHAPTER 6

Violins come in many sizes.

1/16   1/8   1/4   1/2

3/4   7/8   4/4

126

TIPBOOK MUSIC FOR KIDS AND TEENS

BORROWING, RENTING, OR BUYING?

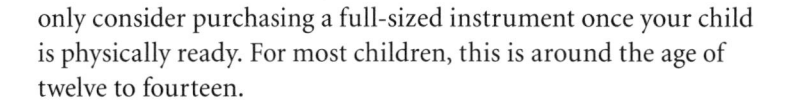

only consider purchasing a full-sized instrument once your child is physically ready. For most children, this is around the age of twelve to fourteen.

More small instruments
There are fractional guitars too, as well as many other instruments that come in down-sized versions for young children (see pages 152–160). For such instruments, renting or leasing usually makes more sense than buying.

The basics
It is impossible to provide a detailed description of the infinite amount of different plans, terms, and conditions you will likely encounter when you decide to lease or rent an instrument. But here are the basics:

- Many **rental plans** are actually rent-to-own plans: The instrument is yours once the periodic payments you've made equal the list price. Note that this list price will usually be higher than what you would have paid had you just bought the instrument outright. This explains why most of these plans are interest free. The profit is in the difference between the standard, discounted street, or 'going' price, and the list price.

- Most of these rent-to-own or **hire-purchase** plans also have an option to buy the instrument before you're fully paid up; if you choose to buy the instrument, your rent paid to date will usually be applied to the instrument.

- With a **lease plan** — also known as a straight rental plan or rent-to-rent plan — you simply keep paying rent until you return the instrument. Rates are usually lower than rent-to-own plan rates. In the long run, however, leasing will typically be more expensive than buying the instrument.

Tips
The following tips and questions may help you decide between buying, renting, and leasing:

- Check the **going price** of the instrument you plan to rent or lease, and calculate how long you would need to rent or lease

CHAPTER 6

it at that price. You don't want to end up paying twice an instrument's price and still not own it.

- Does **the fee** include instrument set-up, maintenance, finance or bank charges, and delivery to your home or your child's school? If not, how much extra will these services cost?
- Is **insurance** included, and if so, does it cover damage, theft, and loss?
- Is there a school **pickup service** for instruments that need repair?
- Do you get a **replacement instrument** if yours needs maintenance?
- Do you have to pay an **origination fee**, an application fee, or a deposit? These costs are usually non-refundable; they often can be applied to the rental, however.
- Is there a **reconditioning fee**, a stocking fee, or a depreciation fee when you return the instrument?
- See if the plan allows your child to **switch instruments**, either to an instrument within the same family (e.g., from one string instrument to another) or to a completely different one (e.g., from guitar to saxophone).
- Are you sure you're not **obliged to buy** the instrument at the end of the plan?
- Find out if you're **allowed to buy** the instrument at any time (referred to as 'buying out the contract'), and if so, what the financial conditions are. A store may offer you a discount on the unpaid balance, or apply a percentage of your paid-up rent to the price of the instrument (List price or street price? Check!) Percentages vary from store to store, typically anywhere from thirty to fifty percent.
- Can the rent you've paid to date also be applied towards **another instrument** (of the same or another family) than the one you contracted to rent?
- Some stores rent instruments on a month-to-month basis; others have a **three-month minimum**, and some rent instruments per semester or school year.

BORROWING, RENTING, OR BUYING?

- If the instrument is rented on a **school-year basis**, what about the summer holidays? There are instrument suppliers who offer rent-free summer months if you sign up to rent for the upcoming school year.
- What about a **discount** if you rent two or three instruments from the same store?
- Final tip: **Always read the fine print**, and ask around before you decide.

Buy back
As an alternative to renting, some stores have a buy-back option. If you return the instrument within a specified period of time, the store buys it back for a percentage of the original purchase price (e.g., 70% within six months, 50% within two years, and so on). *Tip:* The purchase price is often lower than what you'd end up paying over the term of a rental plan. Another tip: Buy-back plans may allow you to switch to another type of instrument or to a higher quality instrument.

New or pre-rented
Most rented or leased orchestral string instruments will be re-rentals (a.k.a. 'pre-rented instruments') because of reasons mentioned earlier. For most other instruments, you'll probably be offered the choice between new and used ones. Some stores charge a lower rental fee for used instruments (this may vary from less than thirty to more than fifty percent); others charge the same fee, but you pay less when you decide to buy the instrument.

Rental fees
The amount of the rental fee will depend on the price and quality of instrument, the services included (insurance, maintenance, etc.), the finance charge and fees, and so on. As a guideline, you'll pay some twenty to thirty dollars per month for a student-line violin, viola, trumpet, or clarinet. More expensive instruments will have a higher rental price, of course. For example, rental fees for a tenor saxophone or oboe may vary from thirty dollars for a used student-line instrument, to ninety dollars for a higher quality new one.

Oboe.

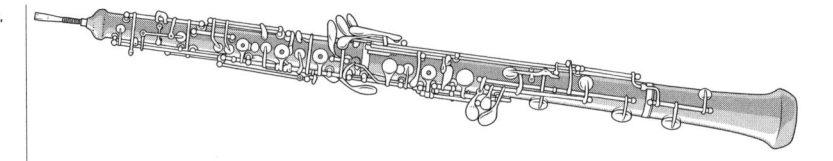

School rental fees
School rental fees are much lower, of course. You may be able to rent an expensive instrument for less than fifty dollars per school year. Many schools provide expensive instruments only (the ones you'd not likely buy yourself, such as bassoons and tubas), or they offer a limited number of instruments of all kinds for families that can't afford to buy or rent elsewhere.

BUYING

In the long run, buying an instrument outright will cost you less than renting one. Buying an instrument also shows your children that you believe in their musical aspirations, and actually owning an instrument may be a great motivator for them.

Discounts
Stores have different ways to make buying attractive. In addition to a buy-back plan, you may be offered a discount if you buy outright, or an even bigger discount if you pay with cash or a check rather than using a credit card. Just like any other store, music stores also have special offers, sales, and so on. Instruments and accessories are often offered below their suggested retail prices. And of course, music stores also sell music books, accessories and all kinds of gadgets that can make playing more fun, and that make great gifts for your child.

Music stores
Basically, there are three types of music stores:
- **Large chain stores** have lots of instruments on display and in stock. They often have soundproof rooms for trying out

BORROWING, RENTING, OR BUYING?

instruments, as well as other services. These stores either focus on combo instruments (acoustic and electric guitars, drums, keyboards, and so on) or they have a large range of band and/or orchestral instruments as well.

- **Local music stores**, often family-owned, usually have a smaller stock — which can actually make choosing an instrument much easier. Service is typically more personal, which adds value to the cost of their instruments, since they usually (!) can't beat the prices of chain stores. Most local music stores are so-called 'full-line' stores, carrying a wide variety of instruments. The general focus is on low- and medium-budget products.

- **Specialty stores** sell only instruments of a particular musical family or group of related families: drums, guitars, strings, woodwinds, pianos, and so on. These types of stores typically offer both specialized information and instruments in a wide range of prices. Violin makers (a.k.a. luthiers) may also sell and rent student-line violins, violas, cellos, and double basses.

Online and mail order companies

You can also buy musical instruments and accessories online or by mail order — a great option if there are no music stores in your area. Online and mail-order stores may be able to offer very attractive pricing as their operating costs are lower due to low overhead. However, they can't offer one-on-one personal service nor advise you on your favorite instrument, strings, sticks, heads, and other accessories (other than by phone), and you can't just walk in for instrument repair (it can, however, be shipped, which takes time and money, while many of these 'problems' can be solved in a minute if you get a knowledgeable in-store salesperson to take a look). Also, it is impossible to play and compare instruments, and this remains the best way to decide which guitar, saxophone, or violin to buy. That said, you can usually return an instrument you don't like within a certain period of time and get your money back.

Which store?

The more instruments a store has on display, the harder it will be to make a choice. On the other hand, as selecting instruments is mostly a matter of comparing their sound, feel, and playability,

CHAPTER 6

a wide selection gives you a greater basis on which to make your decision. It's important to find a store with salespeople who clearly enjoy their work and know what they're talking about. *Tip:* Ask friends, family, and your child's music teacher for suggestions on which music stores in the area you might visit (note that some organizations do not allow their teachers to give such advice). Some other things to look at:

- Is there an **in-house repair shop**?
- Do you get a **replacement instrument** if yours needs maintenance?
- Do they stock **method books** and other educational materials, or will they order them for you?
- Does the store offer private and/or group **lessons**?
- Do you get **help and advice** on assembly, tuning, and maintenance of the instrument?
- Is **parking** easy and inexpensive?

Expert ears

No two guitars are exactly alike, even if they're of the same brand and type — and that goes for all instruments with the exception of digital models, such as keyboards. There may be subtle differences in timbre (e.g., one violin sounds a tad darker than the other), which isn't of real importance for beginner's instruments. But out of ten 'identical' saxophones, one or more may play a little easier, or be better in tune than the others — and that's something your child will appreciate. Making such comparisons requires a good player, so if you don't play the instrument yourself, try to bring along someone who does. If that's not possible, visit a store with salespeople on staff who can play the instruments for you.

NEW OR SECONDHAND?

Most musical instruments last for a long time, and you can often buy a used intermediate-quality instrument for what you would

BORROWING, RENTING, OR BUYING?

have paid for a new student model. Buying second-hand usually does take more time, effort, and expertise, however.

Privately or in a store?
Purchasing a used instrument from a private party may be less expensive than buying the same model from a store. One of the advantages of buying a used instrument from a retailer, however, is that you can go back if you have questions or problems. Chances are the instrument has been checked and adjusted before being sold to you, and the store may offer you a limited warranty to back its dependability. Also, you may be able to choose between a number of models in stock, and in some cases you can even exchange the instrument you bought for a different one within a certain period of time. A good dealer will sell at a competitive price, whereas private sellers might ask way too much — either because they don't know any better, or because they think that you don't.

An expert
Bringing along an experienced player is even more important if you're buying second-hand from a private party. Without their expert advice, you might turn down a shoddy-looking but otherwise valuable instrument, or get saddled with one that looks great but doesn't sound or play well. Tips:

- A used five-hundred dollar instrument could easily require an additional five-hundred dollars or more in **repairs** before it can be played.

- If you want to be sure you're not paying too much, **get the instrument appraised** first. An expert technician or salesperson can tell you what it's worth, whether it needs any work done, and what that work should cost you.

- If the seller is unwilling to allow an appraisal, that could be **a warning sign** of serious problems.

Online?
The Internet is a great source for used gear, but buying a musical instrument that you haven't seen or heard could prove hazardous. You could luck out and find a great instrument for far below its

CHAPTER 6

market value, but you could just as easily end up paying lots of money for an unplayable piece of equipment.

Age

Is it important to know the age of a used instrument? That depends on the type of instrument. For many instruments, age doesn't really make a difference in terms of sound, intonation, or playability, as long as they're in good shape.

- **Violins, violas, cellos and double basses** can last for hundreds of years (and often become worth more as they get older!).

- **Pianos** typically last fifty years or more.

- **Drums and guitars** can still be in mint condition after dozens of years.

- Older saxophones and other **wind instruments** often don't play as well as newer instruments. Also, pre-World War II wind instruments may have a deviant standard tuning, rendering them useless for ensemble work with modern horns.

- **Digital instruments** such as keyboards and digital pianos become obsolete faster than most acoustic instruments as sounds, connections, and options continue to improve and expand (much like cell phones and cameras). Although they may be out-of-date, they're still playable, of course, and you may be able to buy last year's still-great model for relatively little money!

For more details and technical tips on buying second-hand instruments, please consult your relevant Tipbook (see pages 239–243).

Paperwork

If you do buy second-hand, ask the seller for any associated documents they might have: the original receipt, the manual, brochures, and so on. These documents are often fun to read, and they can helpful if you decide to resell the instrument later on. Also, find out if and when the instrument has undergone professional checkups and maintenance. For pianos, this should include tuning. A piano that hasn't been tuned for years may be very hard or impossible to tune.

BORROWING, RENTING, OR BUYING?

Tuning a piano.

Stepping up
If your child is ready to move on to a better instrument, you may try to trade in the old one, sell it privately (this may be more profitable, but it usually takes more time), or keep it as a spare.

ADDITIONAL COSTS

Apart from lesson fees and the rent or purchase of an instrument, there are some additional costs that you need to be aware of, ranging from sticks and strings to maintenance and tuning, band fees, and sheet music. Below are some examples. More details can be found in Tipbooks on the various instruments shown on pages 239–243. Music stands, metronomes, and tuners were discussed on pages 84–87.

Strings, reeds, heads, and so on
String instruments periodically need new strings. Guitar strings

CHAPTER 6

cost less than violin or cello strings, but the latter last (much) longer. Drummers need new drum heads and new drum sticks from time to time, and reed instruments require new reeds once in while. For beginners, most of these costs will be reasonable: A ten-dollar set of guitar strings easily lasts a year; beginning drummers are unlikely to go through many pairs of sticks or a drum head every single day (although some hard-hitting pros do, at some five to ten dollars for a pair of sticks!); saxophone and clarinet reeds typically cost between a dollar fifty to three dollars each, and they may last anywhere from a couple of days or less, to a month or more. Bassoon and oboe reeds cost more, but last longer.

Maintenance

Costs for repairs and professional maintenance can be kept to a minimum by taking proper care of an instrument. Daily maintenance usually takes little time and even less money. In many cases, a cleaner and a cloth are all you need. Consult your child's teacher, your dealer, or a Tipbook on your instrument for instructions and tips.

Daily maintenance: a swab or a pad saver is used to dry the inside of the saxophone.

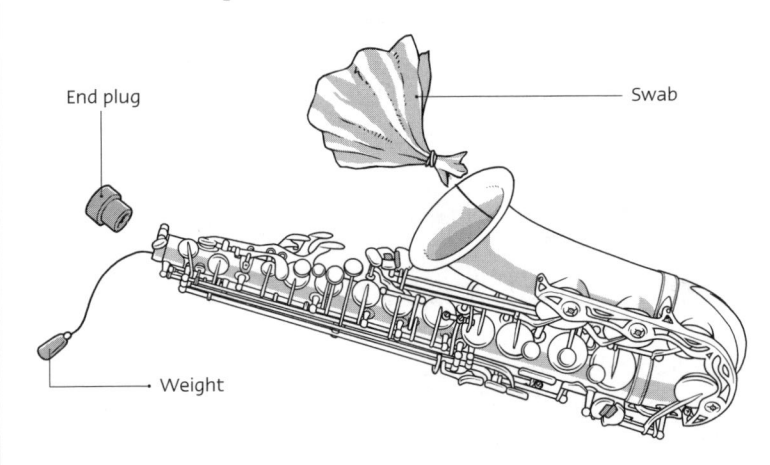

End plug

Swab

Weight

Wind instruments

Clarinets, saxophones, and other woodwinds need an annual COA (Cleaning, Oiling, Adjustment), which typically costs some fifty to seventy-five dollars. A complete overhaul is required for both woodwinds and brasswinds once every few years — the frequency and cost dependent on how well the instrument is maintained

BORROWING, RENTING, OR BUYING?

and how frequently it is played. Daily maintenance requires a very small investment in one or more special brushes, oil, and cleaners.

Pianos
Pianos need to be tuned two to three times a year at some sixty to a hundred dollars for each tuning. More extensive maintenance (e.g., checking and adjusting the instrument's action and pedals) is less frequent.

Orchestral strings
Orchestral string instruments require some maintenance daily (basically cleaning with a dry cloth), and many string players have their instruments checked annually. Rosin cakes are very affordable, starting at around three dollars, and last a long time. The hair of a string player's bow needs to be replaced every few years, which should be done only by a professional.

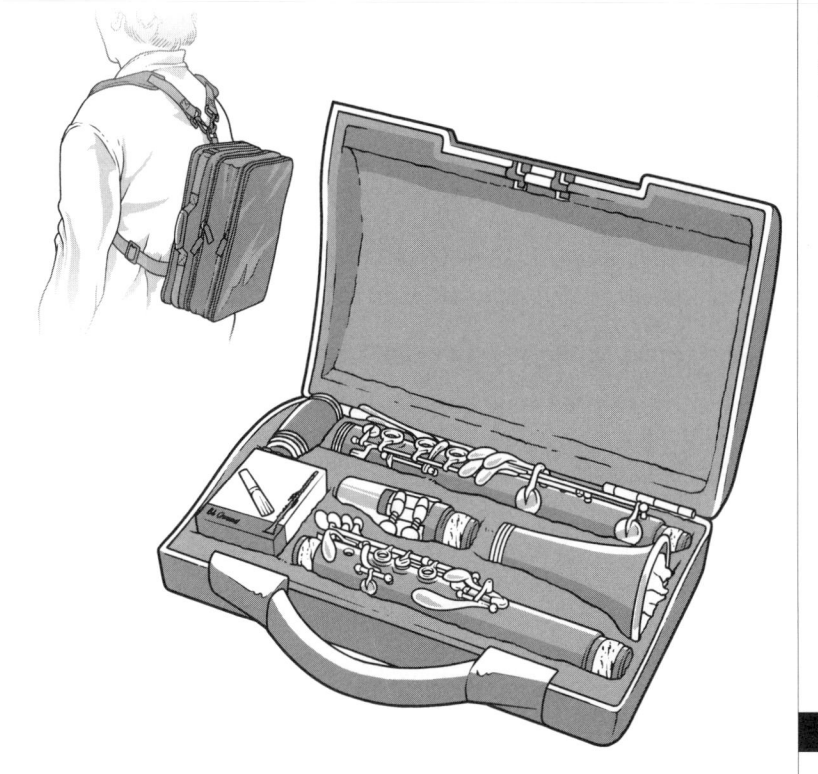

Gig bag with backpack straps; clarinet case.

TIPBOOK MUSIC FOR KIDS AND TEENS

CHAPTER 6

Drums and guitars
Drum sets and guitars can function properly for many years without any professional attendance. Most special instrument cleaners are low-cost and last a long time, and some household cleaners may work fine too. Never use abrasive or agressive cleaners, though!

Cases and covers
Always find out if a case or cover is included in the price of your child's instrument. You can do without one as long as the instrument doesn't leave the house, but even so, such protection is critical to guarding your investment against dust, dirt, and damage.

Sheet music
Your investment in sheet music may go up as your child progresses, but for the first couple of years they'll be limited to the few books specified by their teachers, usually at some ten to twenty dollars per book. Note that most serious books will take your child several months at least.

Insurance
Your home owners' policy may or may not cover damage, loss, or theft of your musical instruments; check the text carefully. If the instrument leaves the house — albeit for a weekly lesson, a rehearsal, or a concert — you'll probably need additional insurance to have it covered while on the road.

Serial number
To get an instrument insured you will usually need to state its serial number, if provided, and some other details. You can store these data on pages 232–233. Insurance companies often require an appraisal report and proof of purchase as well.

Band and orchestra fees
Bands and orchestras often charge a fee to cover the costs of uniforms, transportation, equipment, music, competition entry fees, operations, and so on. Annual fees typically run between twenty and one hundred dollars. There may be extra fees for summer camps or tours.

BORROWING, RENTING, OR BUYING?

> ### On the road
> Even when an instrument is well insured, it's better to prevent it from getting lost. Here are a few tips to share with your child:
>
> - Don't put your instrument on the **luggage shelf** of a car, under the rear window — especially not on a hot day.
>
> - Don't leave your instrument in an **unattended car.**
>
> - All kinds of things — including musical instruments — get left behind in the luggage racks of buses, trains, and subways. Tip: Always **keep hold of your instrument**.
>
> - If you still leave your instrument behind somewhere, you're more likely to get it back if your **name, (email) address, and phone number** are listed inside your case or bag.

Exam fees
Exam fees vary from board to board, and higher-level exams are more expensive than beginner's exams. Prices range from around fifty dollars for the latter to a hundred or two hundred dollars for the highest (non-professional) grades. Fees for theory exams are usually lower — say, from around thirty to fifty dollars.

All in all?
The total annual cost of funding your budding musician depends on many things: instrument rental, lessons (usually the costliest element), and maintenance can easily add up to a thousand to fifteen hundred dollars per year. But you may end up paying less if you borrow an instrument and/or enroll your child in group lessons through school, for example; expect to pay more if the route you choose includes a highly qualified teacher, a high-quality, high-maintenance instrument, and all kinds of additional fees. Note that you may be able to help out at band or orchestra events in lieu of your child's annual ensemble fees and that there are financial aid options for families with demonstrated financial

CHAPTER 6

needs. School music teachers and band directors should be able to inform you where to go for information on this.

7

Which Instrument?

For many children, the question of which instrument to play is something they don't need to mull over — they already know. But what if your child doesn't? The following chapter looks at this topic from a number of different perspectives and questions various preconceived ideas on instrument selection.

CHAPTER 7

If children express a strong desire to play a certain instrument, you should probably trust their instincts. If their heart is in it, they'll be more motivated to stick with it. Conversely, playing the 'wrong' instrument is probably one of the main reasons that children quit their music programs or private lessons. In other words, the answer to the question, 'Which instrument?' can be of crucial importance to the longevity of your child's musical ambitions.

But...
That said, even children who passionately expressed a desire to play a certain instrument may give up playing after a couple of months, and kids who were assigned an instrument because it was the only one available could end up falling in love with it and becoming successful professionals. Still, if you want your children to enjoy playing music, you'll improve your (and their) chances by at least letting them have a say in choosing their instrument.

Sound and looks
Children often choose an instrument because they like its sound, its looks, or both. Exposing them to music — preferably live music in a wide variety of styles, including the ones you don't like yourself — allows them to identify instruments and develop a preference. Anything else you do to encourage your child musically will help, as discussed in Chapter 3.

A friend
Children may also pick an instrument because a friend plays it and they want to join in, or because they're drawn to an artist who plays that particular instrument. Though you may worry that choosing by such criteria may not be the best way to go about it, they're not the worst criteria either. The same goes for kids who want to join their friends' garage band and simply start playing the lacking instrument, be it bass, drums, or guitar.

Availability
Having instruments around the house may definitely inspire a child's desire. Many children start playing an instrument because it happens to be available. If they do, rather than being pressured to play it because it's there, this typically indicates a match.

WHICH INSTRUMENT?

Siblings
Younger children may be inspired by the instrument an older sibling plays. Some will argue that you should dissuade them from playing the same instrument in order to avoid sibling rivalry — but this type of competition is typically unavoidable. Looking at the bright side, if they get along well, the older brother or sister can even help guide the younger one. *Tip:* While the idea of a family ensemble might sound appealing, your children may not appreciate being assigned an instrument based solely on the musical needs of the ensemble that you have in mind.

Friends and relatives
Getting hands-on experience with different instruments can help a child make a more informed choice. Ask friends and relatives who play — amateurs, professionals, and anyone in between — to demonstrate their instruments for your children. They even might be willing to let them have a go at it.

Exploratory courses
Some schools offer exploratory courses allowing children to try various instruments. This teaches children some very basic techniques, and they may even get to do some ensemble work that incorporates all the available instruments, preferably in different styles of music. This is probably the best option for children who want to play but can't seem to choose an instrument. It's also a great way to open new horizons for kids who have already made their choice.

Guidance
Guiding your children as they choose their instruments requires little more than a bit of common sense. Some examples? If your child loves to sing, but also wants to play an instrument, the guitar or piano are good choices as both instruments can be played to accompany the vocal performance. Solitary learners may like these instruments as well, but note that they can make them even more solitary.

Instruments and styles
Some instruments will unavoidably guide your child toward

CHAPTER 7

a certain musical style. The oboe and bassoon are hardly used outside the field of classical music, and some types of brasswinds are only used in wind bands, for example. And if your child has a deep love of classical music, you may want to suggest the clarinet over the saxophone, as there is less classical repertoire for the latter, a relatively young instrument.

New directions
That said, it's better to be open to what musical direction could be taken, rather than limiting your child to the paths that have been followed before. The flute is not a typical rock instrument, but it has been used in such bands, just like harps and violins, for example.

Whatever instrument
For children who simply love being part of the band or school orchestra, their instrument choice may not matter that much; you might even suggest that they choose one of the instruments needed most. Even professional musicians sometimes take this route: If music is their livelihood, and playing the bass guitar just happens to be lucrative because there are not too many bassists available, they go play the bass guitar.

An electric bass guitar.

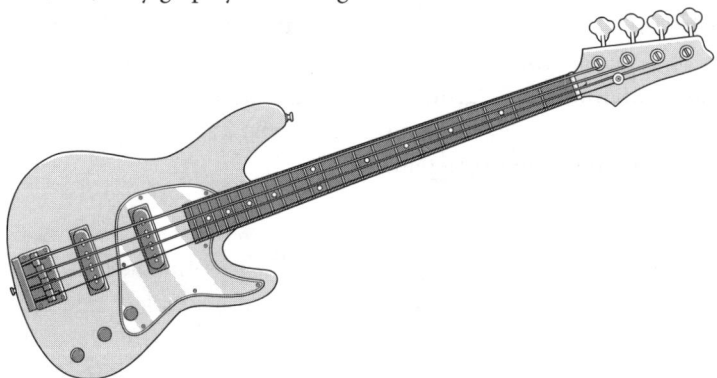

Reading, writing, piano playing
Some parents simply make music lessons a non-debatable part of their children's upbringing. Just like their children have to go to school and learn reading, writing, and arithmetic at one point, they require them to take piano lessons for one, two, or three

WHICH INSTRUMENT?

years, and then allow them to choose another instrument, or to quit. Learning piano provides a solid foundation for learning other instruments, so if you take this approach, this would be a good choice.

Switching instruments

No matter what the reason that children end up with whatever instrument they do, chances are they'll want to switch after a couple of years, or even sooner. Even adults tend to change their minds, and children are a lot more likely to develop new preferences, to discover new sounds, or to just want to change because they want to. Young violinists may want to switch to the electric guitar when they get into their teens, for example. Forcing them to stick with violin may compel them to quit, while allowing them to explore the guitar could enrich their musical education.

Within the same family

However, children cannot effectively progress if they switch instruments every year. If your child ends up not liking the instrument they chose, first suggest that he or she switches to an instrument within the same instrument family (from flute to saxophone, rather than guitar, for example). Why? Because when they do, they'll be able to apply so much of what they've already learned to the new instrument. Chances are, however, that children who have grown to really dislike a woodwind won't choose an instrument from that same family. They'll often want something completely different.

> **Failure or success**
>
> Many well-known musicians switched instruments when they were younger. Some because they liked another instrument better; others because they had trouble learning their first instrument (such as the well-known drummer who started on cello but was made to stop because he couldn't count!). This also addresses the concern that you can't succeed on one instrument if you failed on another: You most certainly can!

CHAPTER 7

Success
Desire is one of the best motivators. A child who desires to play a certain instrument will usually succeed at it, especially if success is measured in terms of enjoyment and the motivation to persist, rather than in terms of reaching a certain standard. So even if it seems as though the odds are against your child's instrument choice, you could definitely consider to give in and let their desires prevail. But what if your child has genuine limitations? For example, can you learn to play the trumpet with a cleft lip and palate? Although perhaps not the easiest of endeavors, there's a least one professional trumpeter who did, simply because he wanted to. There's more on the physical aspects of choosing an instrument on pages 148–152.

ASSIGNING INSTRUMENTS

Band directors need a certain number of each instrument for a full ensemble, and instrument assignment for school bands and orchestras can be more about matching students to the required instruments than about what the student may prefer. After all, you can't have a wind band with twelve drummers and two clarinet players.

Tests
Some schools use aptitude tests to determine which instrument would be best for your child. These tests are often followed by a (classroom or individual) demonstration of the various instruments for students and their parents. Some schools ask the students to choose their top three favorite instruments from the band's line up, and then assign them one of the three.

Even teeth, pointed chin
Matching students to instruments is a skill that requires a great deal of attention for the student and his or her needs. It's definitely not as simple as some lists seem to suggest: 'Even teeth, a pointed chin, and medium lips? A clarinetist. Same features but a round chin? The trombone.' There's more on this on pages 148–152.

Grades
Some schools select particular students for 'difficult' instruments (typically the oboe, bassoon, and French horn) because they get good grades. However, there doesn't seem to be any evidence of a relationship between academic performance and one's talent for these — or any other — instruments. Other schools make the 'popular' instruments available only to students with the highest scores as a way of limiting the number of applicants, or they prohibit certain instruments from students with a history of academic or behavioral problems. As a parent, it is good to be aware of such rules.

TALENTS AND ABILITIES

If children really want to play an instrument, lack of talent or natural ability can usually be made up for in sheer desire, and their ability may increase as they go. In other words, you can advise a kid with poor foot-hand coordination not to play the drums, but you could also see this as an opportunity for that child to improve this type of coordination — especially if that instrument is the one favored by the child. If you see your child putting in a lot of hard work without any success, you can always suggest to switch instruments. Some teachers may also suggest a different instrument if they feel that the switch would better benefit your child's specific talents, motor skills, or musical preferences. If you present the proposed switch to your child as something that he or she will benefit from, the answer will probably be yes.

Relative pitch
All children have the ability to develop a musical ear, to some degree at least. And they can definitely improve their relative pitch, which enables them to hear whether they're playing in tune. This skill is important for everyone who plays an instrument that requires you to control the exact pitch yourself — from orchestral strings to brasswinds and woodwinds — and for all players who

CHAPTER 7

tune their own instruments. Even drummers need a sense of pitch if they want to make their drums sound perfect. (Tuning a set of drums is a lot harder than tuning a guitar or a violin!)

Perfect pitch
Whether you can actually be trained in or develop perfect pitch or absolute pitch (the ability to recognize and name a pitch without any reference) is debatable. People who have perfect pitch aren't always glad they do — it's horrible if you have to play a piano that's just below or above standard tuning, for example.

PHYSICAL FEATURES

Should trumpeters have thin lips? Not really, as you can tell by simply looking at some of the greatest players. Should violinists have medium-sized hands? Again, not really.

All shapes and sizes
Selecting an instrument based on the potential player's physique is a hazardous affair. You simply can't look at people's dimensions and tell them what to play based on that assessment. Though it is undeniably true that certain physical features can make certain instruments a bit easier or harder to play, it is also true that a kid's desire to play a certain instrument can overcome almost all of their physical and other features and characteristics. One look at the violin section of a symphony orchestra is enough to tell you that violinists come in all shapes and sizes, and the same goes for all other instrumentalists.

Aware
Still, it's good to know that some physical characteristics could get in the way or slow your child down. Teachers and band directors are usually aware of such factors and will pinpoint, perhaps even solve the problem before the child gets too discouraged and quits (the real reason possibly unknown to them or you). Following are some random thoughts and facts on the subject.

WHICH INSTRUMENT?

Lips

Lips are mainly important for brasswind players and flutists. Here's what you can tell your child:

- The **size of your** lips has no impact on your ability to play larger or smaller brasswinds. The texture of your lips does, to some extent, but this kind of determination should be left to a professional. Soft, supple lips can make playing brasswind instruments with large mouthpieces easier to play, while having tougher lips may be a good thing for trumpeters.

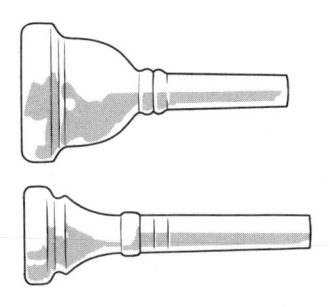

Larger brasswind instruments have larger mouthpieces. The upper one is a trombone mouthpiece, the lower is a trumpet mouthpiece.

- All brasswinds require that your lips meet properly, so you can create the **lip valve** (a.k.a. 'lip reed') you need to generate sound. A short upper lip is no problem as long as it's compensated for by a longer lower lip, for example.

- To enjoy playing a brasswind instrument, you need a mouthpiece that **suits your physique**. Given the right mouthpiece, you can basically play any brass instrument regardless of your type of lips. Trying nothing but a standard mouthpiece may steer talented students away from instruments they really like.

- **Flutists** depend on their lips too, and much has been said regarding lip shapes that make playing this instrument hard, or even impossible. However, with enough attention, a good teacher, and a motivated student, most of these and many other 'problems' can be overcome rather easily. For example, a teardrop-shaped upper lip tends to split the flutist's air column, which can be a problem, but changing the relative position of the lips — rolling the upper lip out, or simply repositioning the flute — may be enough to solve this issue.

CHAPTER 7

Teeth

The shape and size of a child's teeth can play a role too, but again, it's always best to let children have a go at the instrument they want to play. Some kids with irregular, large front teeth play the flute effortlessly, while another kid with 'perfect flute teeth' may not be able to produce the faintest sound on the instrument.

- Chapter 3 discussed the influence of **braces** and whether it's important to have your permanent teeth before playing a wind instrument; see pages 59–63.

- For flutists, a **gap between the front teeth** may cause loss of pressure. A dentist can adjust the gap.

- A profound **underbite or overbite** can make playing a wind instrument quite hard. Choosing the right mouthpiece can help alleviate this problem for brass players. The same goes for saxophonists and clarinetists, and there are all kind of special head joints for flutists available.

Lefties

Left-handed players can play any instrument a right-handed player can, and most instruments do not come in 'left-handed' editions. Some do — but there's a usually a but:

- Left-handed **guitars and bass guitars** are available — but in smaller numbers than right-handed instruments, and they're often more expensive.

- Left-handed **drummers** and Latin percussionists can simply re-arrange their instrument to accommodate themselves — but this makes it harder to use someone else's set, such as their teacher's, or a drum set at a jam session.

- At a price, **orchestral string instruments** can be adapted — but players who play 'the wrong way around' may not be welcome in an orchestra, simply because of the visual aspect.

Double-jointed fingers

Children with double-jointed fingers (joint laxity, hyper mobility) may have problems with certain instruments such as the guitar, the piano, the flute, or the oboe. Special exercises and proper

WHICH INSTRUMENT?

guidance and advice from a dedicated, knowledgeable teacher often helps. Also, professional players with hyper mobility often suffer less from aches and pains than those without this condition!

Respiratory problems

Contrary to popular belief, children with respiratory problems can actually benefit from learning to play a wind instrument. Many wind players have been advised to play this type of instrument *because* they had asthma!

Physical impairments

There are specialists who can adapt instruments to a wide variety of physical impairments, ranging from special guitar stands to one-of-a-kind wind instruments for players with a missing hand or missing fingers, and vertical or 'swan neck' flutes for children whose disability prevents them from holding a regular flute properly. *Tip:* The trumpet is one of the very few instruments that can be played with one hand without adaptations. Another tip: Using the 'full keyboard' mode on a home keyboard allows a single-handed player to play both the accompaniment and the melody or a solo! For more information on these and many other solutions, you may consult specialized instrument makers or the organizations on page 227.

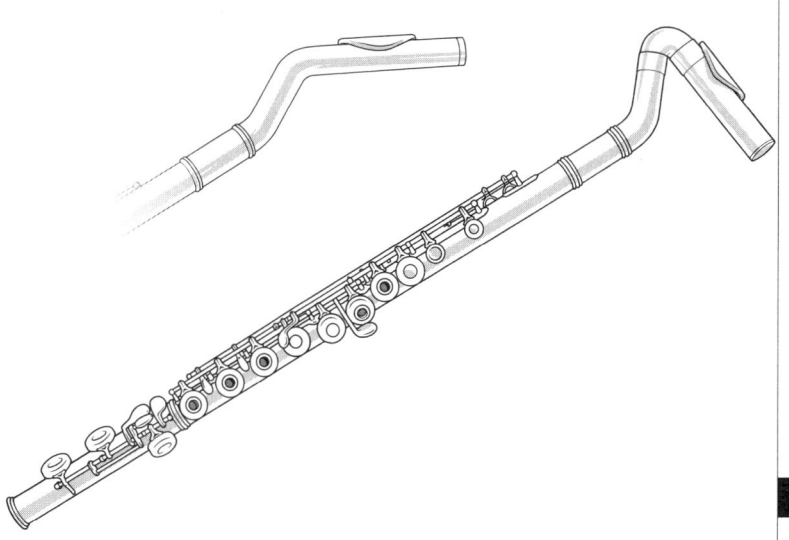

An ergonomically adapted 'swan neck' flute (Flutelab).

CHAPTER 7

Size

When it comes to physical size, most kids are capable of playing any instrument by ten or eleven years of age. Around that same age, most school bands and orchestras begin recruiting new musicians. For younger kids, there are various special smaller-sized instruments available (see below), and some instruments can simply be adapted to their size. In other words, kids don't need long arms to play the trombone, or be a giant to start playing the double bass. Many adults also play down-sized instruments, from short scale bass guitars and Concert-type steel-string guitars to ⅞ violins. A full-sized double bass is too big for most adult bass players; they usually play a ¾ size.

DOWN-SIZED INSTRUMENTS AND AGES

Why do kids as young as four often start on the violin? Because it's one of the few instruments available in such small sizes. There are also fractional violas and cellos for kids this age, as covered on pages 125–127. There are many other down-sized instruments, but they're usually intended for slightly older kids. Some of the better and lesser-known examples are listed on the following pages. Guidelines on the age at which children could start playing various instruments are included. Do keep in mind that they're no more than suggestions, however: Your eight-year-old may very well be taller than your neighbor's ten-year-old. Please note that some of the instruments listed below may not (yet) be available in your country.

Chapter 9
More information on the full sized versions of the instruments in the next section can be found in Chapter 9, *The Instruments*.

Wind instruments
The sooner you begin on an instrument, the better it generally is. The main reason kids can't start playing a wind instrument until around the age of six or seven is that these instruments

WHICH INSTRUMENT?

are too big and too heavy. Kids need wind instruments that are lightweight, easy to play, and possibly feature fewer keys than the 'adult' versions. Unfortunately, the number of down-sized wind instruments is still quite limited, and these perfectly viable instruments are currently made by small companies only. Even though numerous kids enjoy these instruments very much (they don't have to wait to play the oboe until they're eleven anymore!), not all teachers are fully convinced of their value. This may not change until the leading makers of larger wind instruments start producing down-sized versions, allowing them to gain wider acceptance.

Supports and harnesses
Neck straps and harnesses are available for making wind instruments easier to play for young children (and for adults, too!). However, because they don't reduce the weight, but rather redistribute it, these instruments may still be too heavy for your child.

Recorder
There's one wind instrument that needs no down-sizing: the recorder. Children can play this instrument as soon as they are capable of closing all the toneholes, which is typically when they're five or six. The recorder is also very affordable (forty or fifty dollars can get you a good instrument); it hardly needs maintenance, and a child can learn to play a few simple songs in no time. Playing the recorder also helps develop the fine motor skills you need to play any other instrument, and it can be played alone, in recorder ensembles, or accompanied by a piano, for example. Being a relatively 'easy' instrument, children can focus on learning to read music as they play the recorder, experiencing how written notes translate to pitches. For these and other reasons, the recorder is often considered a great instrument for all budding musicians, and especially for aspiring woodwind players. However, children who are old and big enough are usually better off starting right away with the instrument of their choice. The fingering of the recorder is somewhat similar to the saxophone or flute fingerings, but fingering is a relatively easy thing to learn. Also, all other woodwinds demand a very different embouchure (how to use the muscles in and around your mouth to blow the instrument).

CHAPTER 7

Flute

Though relatively light and small, the flute is not the easiest instrument to hold. A number of flute makers produce special junior models that feature offset finger buttons and extended keys that decrease the wide spacing of the regular instrument's keys, while a curved head joint brings all levers and keys closer to the player. Some teachers dislike flutes with curved head joints because they may induce bad posture. Also, balancing the instrument is said to become a little harder. As the curved head joint leaves little room to grab the instrument by its non-keyed parts, assembling the instrument is a bit harder too. Alternatively, teachers have children start on very affordable, plastic keyless flutes, or on the E♭ flute, which is a little smaller than the regular concert flute. Student models of this particular flute are not as common as regular student flutes, however. The piccolo, the flute family's smallest member, is not suited for beginning players as it's not only harder to play; it's also harder to play in tune.

A keyless plastic flute and a children's flute.

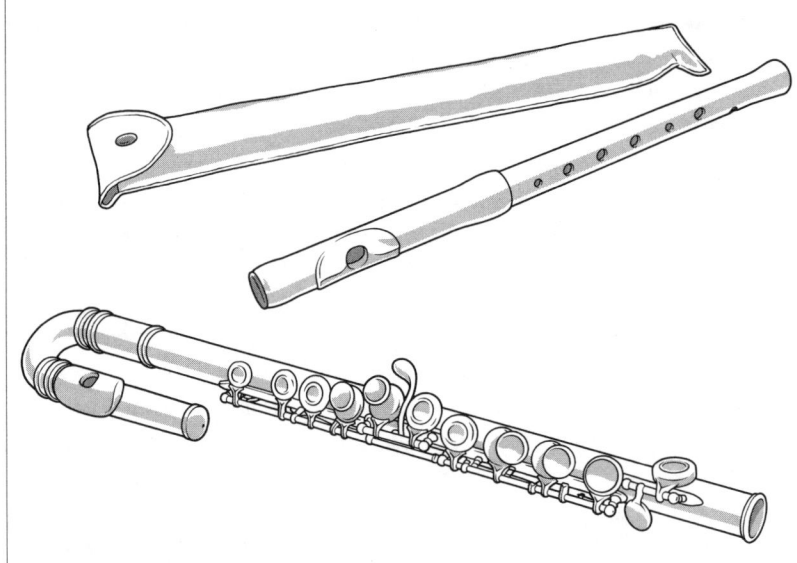

Saxophone

Most beginning saxophone players start on alto saxophone when they're around ten years of age. At that age, the larger tenor is usually too big and too heavy, and the smaller soprano saxophone is typically harder to play. If the alto is still too big, aspiring sax players are usually advised to start on clarinet, a different, yet very similar instrument with the same type of mouthpiece. Switching from the clarinet to the saxophone is easier than the other way around.

Clarinet

Most teachers advise children not to start the clarinet before they're eight to ten years of age. Some companies make special clarinets for younger children, such as the Kinderklari and Clarinova clarinets. The latter, designed for children from age five or six, weighs about one-third that of a regular clarinet, has a simplified mechanism, is more durable, and needs less maintenance. Not all teachers endorse these instruments, but if your youngster loves the sound of the clarinet, find a teacher who does: They're the ones who don't believe in asking a child to wait for a couple years. *Tip:* Some private teachers have younger kids start on the E♭ clarinet, a smaller, higher pitched voice of the family. There is a much wider selection of affordable student model B♭ clarinets available, though.

Saxonett

The Saxonett is a child's instrument designed for aspiring clarinet and saxophone players, consisting of a wooden, recorder-like body without keys, and a clarinet mouthpiece.

Oboe

Many kids start on the oboe when they're nine to eleven years of age. Their first instrument is usually a plastic one, which weighs less than a wooden oboe. A light reed makes the instrument easier to play. Kids can start playing oboes at a much earlier age, however: The

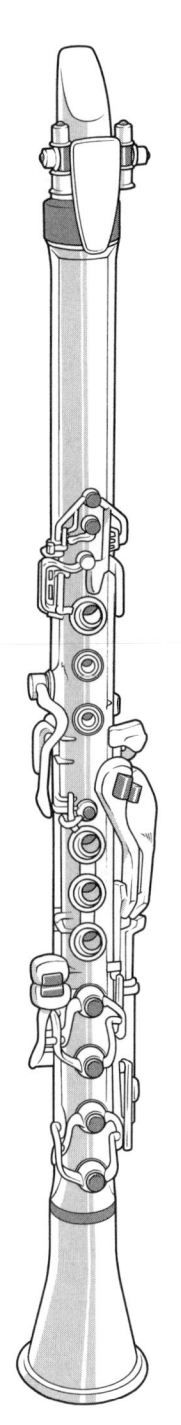

The Jupiter Saxonett.

CHAPTER 7

A children's oboe (Guntram Wolf, Germany).

German Guntram Wolf company, for example, makes oboes with few keys, and even without keys. The latter can be played by children from age six or even younger.

Bassoon
The bassoon is a large instrument that requires quite a large hand span. Children can play the bassoon once they're about the same size as the instrument, which is typically around the age of ten or eleven. For smaller kids, various companies offer bassoons with a covered C-hole. Bassoon makers can also adapt the instrument to smaller hands, but this doesn't reduce the considerable weight of the instrument. Various European companies produce down-sized bassoons that can be played by younger children (e.g., Moosman and Guntram Wolf in Germany, and Bruno Salenson in France).

Trumpet
Pocket trumpets look like very small trumpets, but they're not designed for children. (They actually have the same tube length as a regular trumpet!). Many eight- or nine-year-olds start on the cornet, an instrument that is very similar to the trumpet. It's easier to handle because it's a bit shorter, and easier to play because it requires less air pressure. The even shorter and easier-blown flugelhorn can be offered as an alternative for young kids too.

A pocket trumpet: not designed for children.

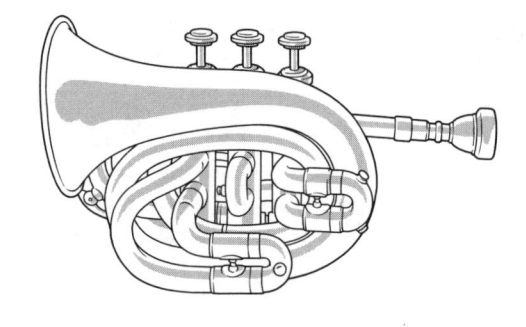

TIPBOOK MUSIC FOR KIDS AND TEENS

Trombone

There are various options for seven- to nine-year-olds who want to play the trombone:

- **Alto trombones** are a bit smaller and lighter than the regular-sized (tenor) trombone.

- The tenor trombone can be fitted with an **extension arm** that allows students with shorter arms to reach the 6th and 7th positions. However, the instrument is still very large and hard to balance if you're small.

- Some companies make special junior or **compact trombones** with shorter slides and other adaptations.

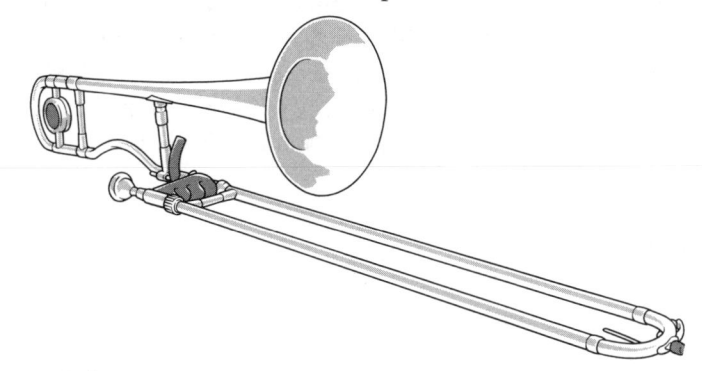

Junior trombone (Jupiter).

French horn

The French horn basically comes in two versions: the single horn, tuned either in B♭ or in F, and the double horn, which can be shifted from B♭ to F with an extra valve. Most players start on a single horn, usually switching to the double horn after one or two years of playing. A few companies make a French horn for children, which is a bit lighter and has a special type of wrap that makes it smaller and thus easier to handle.

Baritone, tenor horn, tuba

Most other brasswinds (e.g., background brass instruments such as the baritone, tenor horn, or tuba) can be played by most kids at age eight or nine. Aspiring tuba players usually start on a smaller background brass instrument, and they can usually switch to tuba around the age of eleven or twelve. *Tip:* There are ¾ and even smaller tubas for children.

CHAPTER 7

Guitar
Acoustic guitars are available in various fractional sizes. The smallest model is typically around three-quarters the size of a standard instrument. (There is no consensus on how to indicate this size. Some companies call it a ½ guitar, others ¼, or even ⅛.) Most smaller guitars have nylon strings, but there are down-sized steel-string ('folk') guitars too, as well as down-sized electric guitars that can be played by most kids around the age of seven. Kids who fall in love with the instrument at an even younger age may start on a ukulele, a four-string family member with Hawaiian roots.

Percussion
Percussion instruments are very accessible; all you have to do is hit or shake them (although playing them musically requires a lot more than that!). This explains why there are so many small percussion instruments for children, ranging from frame drums in all sizes and shapes, to shakers and bongos, tambourines, and xylophones. The choice is yours.

Drums
Toy drum sets should not be confused with higher quality down-sized drum sets, which your child will enjoy much more. Visit a music store for the real thing. Note that junior drum sticks are also available. Regular sticks are way too heavy and too long for young drummers.

Piano and keyboard
The piano is a great instrument to start on. You can watch your hands as you play, all the keys are neatly arranged from the low notes on your left to the high notes on your right, and it's the ideal tool for developing a basic understanding of music, allowing you to play a bass line, chords, and a melody. Therefore it is often considered the perfect instrument to start on, before moving on to another instrument. Being a virtual orchestra on its own, it is used by numerous composers of many styles, and many musicians play it as their secondary instrument. Even though a regular piano keyboard is quite large for most kids' hands, many children start playing this instrument at a very early age, some as young as three or four. The main thing is to find a teacher who is willing to teach

your child at such a young age. Toy pianos come in all shapes and colors, but they're toys, not pianos. The same basically goes for digital home keyboards with down-sized keys.

Harp
As the pedal harp is such an expensive instrument, with prices typically starting around ten thousand dollars, children tend to start with smaller types of harps, such as the Celtic harp (a.k.a. lever harp or folk harp). These harps typically have between thirty-one and forty strings. Celtic harps can be played by most six-year-olds, but they're played by adults too. There are smaller harps for even younger kids.

Accordion
The accordion, known as the poor man's piano until the advent of the home keyboard, is another instrument available in various junior sizes. Again, do note the difference between toy instruments and the real thing. A toy is something you can only play with; an instrument is something you play.

Double bass
Most seven-year-olds can start on a ⅛ or ⅒ double bass. These

> **Making instruments more accessible**
> *There are many ways that teachers can make instruments more accessible to young children. For example, they may use colored stickers on the fingerboard of a violin, indicating the correct positions for the left hand fingers. Similar stickers can be used for guitar or ukulele ('Put your fingers on the blue stickers to play a G-major chord!'). Some use colored stickers on the keys of a piano or a home keyboard to correspond with music notation that uses matching colors. At the same time, other teachers put stickers on the bars of bell sets, which usually have the note names engraved: Hiding these letters helps the student learn to recognize the positions of the bars, rather than reading their note names.*

CHAPTER 7

instruments are some sixteen inches shorter than a regular, adult ¾ double bass (see page 152). Is your child younger than seven? There are four-year-olds playing 'bass' on a ⅛ cello, using special strings that allow for a bass tuning.

GENDER

Even though the number of female drummers, bassists, electric guitarists, and trombonists has increased over the years, children still tend to think of these instruments as being 'for boys.' Likewise, the flute and harp are among the instruments still considered to be mainly 'for girls.' Needless to say, gender should not play a role when it comes to choosing an instrument.

PERSONALITY

It is true that the typical flutist is a different person than the average drummer (assuming that the 'typical' flutist and the average drummers even exist). Also, there may be significant differences in the temperaments of trumpeters and oboists. However, when it comes to choosing instruments, children's personalities should be about as important as the way they look or dress. There are enough kids with pierced eyebrows who love playing Bach to prove this. There are drummers who are sweet and gentle, just as there are bassists (you know, the silent people in the back of the band) with the personality and authority of a sledgehammer. So suggesting that physical or 'aggressive' kids should play 'physical' instruments is probably not as good an idea as suggesting that they join the marching band rather than the orchestra — but maybe they'd be even better off if they would join the orchestra, and then play ball or go boxing to balance things out.

WHICH INSTRUMENT?

EASY INSTRUMENTS?

The piano is one of the easiest instruments to play a scale on: Just press eight white keys in a row, one after the other, and you're done. But is the piano an easy instrument? No. There are no easy instruments, actually. It's just that some instruments are a bit easier to start on. For most kids, the flute is easier to start on than the oboe, though some never get a flute to sound any good. Brass instrumentalists often have a slower start than saxophonists, even though a saxophone with all its keys looks far more complex: Those keys actually make it easier to play different pitches on the instrument, and playing those pitches on a trumpet takes much more practice.

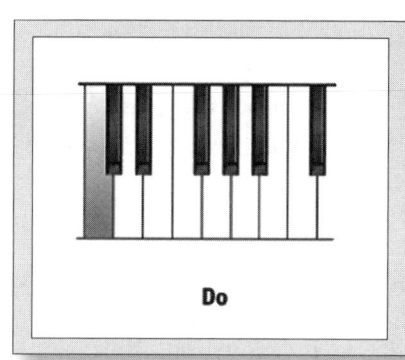

TIPCODE KIDS-003
This Tipcode plays the scale of C major on a piano: eight white keys in a row!

TIPCODE

Difficulties

Each instrument has its own difficulties or challenges. Pianists have to play two parts at the same time, and each hand often plays several keys at once. Organ players also use their left foot for the bass parts, and often their right foot to control their volume. The left hand of a violinist or a classical guitarist does something completely different from what their right hand is doing. Drummers need to develop four-way coordination, using their four limbs simultaneously. And so on...

Rock musicians

Numerous amateur rock guitarists, bassists, and drummers master their instruments to a point where they can perform a host

CHAPTER 7

of songs successfully in a matter of months. By that time they're all set to have tons of fun for years to come. That doesn't make their instruments easy to play, however. It's just that many rock (and country, folk, etc.) songs can be played at an acceptable level without being a virtuoso musician.

The singing voice
The most accessible musical instrument is the singing voice, and the easiest way to be musically active without having to practice daily is to join a school choir, a church choir, a pop choir, or any other type of choir. Still, if you really want to learn how to sing, you can't do so without a voice teacher or a vocal coach. Likewise, serious singers practice daily.

Percussion
Percussion instruments offer instant gratification. After all, you can join a drum circle without any previous experience. That said, there are percussionists who can play a flabbergasting, fascinating five-minute solo on no more than a tambourine — and it took them years of practice.

Keyboard
Home keyboards have built-in, umpteen-piece band or orchestra options that play fully automated beginnings, endings, and accompaniments to your songs, in any style you want, while creating the most complex chords at the push of a button (but there are virtuoso keyboard players who can make each built-in digital sound like a real instrument).

More?
All the instruments detailed above are no more than a few examples of those that offer a relatively easy start. And of course, what a child finds to be 'easy' or 'hard' depends on the child as much as on the instrument. If your child doesn't seem to be making a connection with the instrument of his or her choice, switching instruments may solve things. But first, make sure that their original instrument is in good shape, as discussed on page 120. Don't let a deficient instrument cause your child to feel erroneously incompetent and quit.

WHICH INSTRUMENT?

NOISE, SIZE, PRICE

The number of decibels and contact sound an instrument produces might be a consideration when it comes to choosing an instrument. So might size. Can your kid carry the instrument to school or to lessons, or do they need a car to transport it? Do you have room for an acoustic piano or a drum set, and can it be played without bothering the neighbors? (The latter problem can be solved by buying a digital piano or an electronic drum set, as discussed on pages 92–94.) Instrument prices can be a consideration as well: Harps, French horns, tubas, and baritone saxophones are more expensive than guitars, trumpets, and home keyboards. Your child's school may loan or rent such expensive instruments at a nominal fee, or you can research instrument programs available in your area. The school's music teacher, the band director, or people at the local music store should be able to assist you.

MORE THAN ONE

Many musicians play more than one instrument: either one from the same instrument family, or a completely different one. Some examples:

- Many **sax players** double on the clarinet (and vice versa), or the flute.
- If you're a **trumpeter**, the cornet and the flugelhorn are two instruments within easy technical reach. Switching between larger (background) brass instruments such as the tuba or the baritone is quite easy too. French horn and trombone players rarely choose to play another brasswind.
- Mastering a **keyboard instrument** is a great basis for learning and understanding all other instruments, and it gives you relatively easy access to all other keyboard instruments. That

CHAPTER 7

said, an organ requires a different approach and technique than a piano, for example.

- Some musicians also learn a second instrument to **broaden their scope**. If you play a melody instrument (trumpet, violin, oboe, etc.), you may opt for an instrument that allows you to play chords, or vice versa. And for musicians who're always in the back of the band, such as drummers and bassists, it can be an enlightening experience to learn how to play some of the melodies they're always backing up. The opposite is also true!

- Various instruments are available in **different voices**, such as the saxophone, flute, or clarinet. If you play one of these, the other voices are relatively easy to learn. (Still, most players favor one of those voices!)

TIPCODE

Tipcode KIDS-004
Here you can here the ranges of four of the main clarinet voices: the bass clarinet, the alto clarinet, the B♭ clarinet, and the E♭.

164

TIPBOOK MUSIC FOR KIDS AND TEENS

8

Playing Together

Making music, to most people, means making music together. And practicing, to many people, is something you do to learn an instrument so well that you can join a band, an orchestra, or other ensemble. Here's why playing in a group is so important, followed by an introduction to the main types of musical groups.

CHAPTER 8

Listening to a solo cellist or trumpeter can be fun for a while, but it will be more interesting if they're playing in a band or an orchestra — and the same goes for most other instruments. Drummers and bassists need a band to back up, just like vocalists and soloists need to be backed up, and so on.

Solo?

A few instruments are more suited to playing solo, such as the home keyboard, the piano, and the acoustic guitar. Still, many guitarists prefer playing within some type of ensemble, and playing the piano is often more fun with others, too. In a jazz quartet, for example, or accompanying a violinist, a flutist, or a choir. Some of the main benefits of making music with others were briefly mentioned in Chapter 1. Following are some additional thoughts.

Benefits

First of all, playing in a group provides players with performance opportunities, which is a great motivator. What good is it to practice your oboe or your guitar every day if no one ever hears what you have learned?

Fellow musicians

Even if your child's group does not yet perform, playing in a group can help inspire their practice. They need to be able to play their part so they won't let their fellow musicians and the conductor down, which is a different concern than not performing well for their teacher.

Cooperative environment

Bands and orchestras provide your child with a cooperative environment where they learn to function in both smaller units (e.g., the viola section) and larger groups (the entire orchestra). They also learn how to respond to and take directives from an authority figure (the conductor or band director). The same goes for various athletic activities, of course. What makes music different is that there's nobody to play *against*, which appeals to a different type of motivation. You don't have to be engaged in a competition to have a common goal. And for those who love the competitive element, there are plenty of competing bands!

Better musicians
Playing in a group makes children better musicians, opening their ears and their minds to all the elements that make up music.

Level
Children can usually join a school band or orchestra soon after they started playing, and they will usually find that their fellow musicians play at or around the same level as they do. If things are good, the better players in the group will inspire the newcomers, who will now have something tangible to aim for. However, major differences in playing levels may intimidate children rather than inspire them. Conversely, musically adept children may lose interest if they've surpassed their fellow band members. It may help if advanced players are assigned to a special position in the band, or if they're inspired to help 'lagging' players out. If not, finding another band may be the best solution.

No waiting
The sooner your child joins a group the better, for all the reasons mentioned above. Of course, children who have been playing alone for a couple of years, no matter how talented they are, may still feel a bit intimidated when they discover that the band won't wait for them when they make a mistake or get lost in the music. On the other hand, being a member of a violin section or a brass section can be both inspiring and safe: Hearing all the right notes around you makes it easier for you to play along (and you can often skip a few notes without anyone noticing, too).

Being in the band

Playing in a group means dedicating extra time, both for your child and for yourself. A weekly rehearsal (to which you may have to take your child) is probably the very least you can expect, in addition to the weekly music lesson. Most bands and orchestras rehearse more than once a week. And if there's an upcoming performance, a few extra hours may be added to the schedule, of course.

CHAPTER 8

Time management

Upcoming performances often demand a little extra time management. Make sure you're aware of your child's workload, and encourage children to work ahead on their school assignments so they'll have little to no homework to do on the day of the performance.

Seeking bands and orchestras...

If your child's school has no band or orchestra opportunities, try finding an ensemble by consulting your child's private instructor, your local recreation and community center, your state's art council, the community music school, or the band director of a nearby college. You can also check music stores' bulletin boards and the classified ads in musicians' magazines or your local newspaper, or search online. For everyone who's looking for a band, there's a band looking for them. *Tip:* Many cities have one or more community orchestras and bands.

...or starting one

You or your child may also consider initiating an ensemble yourselves, with or without the assistance of other parents, students, or music teachers. The school may provide a rehearsal room, for example. Opportunities to make music with others can always be found or cultivated, though it may take time to locate people who play the instruments your ensemble is lacking, who are at or around the same level of musicianship as the rest of the group, who have an interest in playing the same style of music, and who are willing to invest the necessary amount of time, and so on. But you don't have to go for a seventy piece wind symphony or a full-blown big band right-away: Playing in a guitar duo, a horn trio, a string quartet, or a jazz quintet will provide your child with most or all of the benefits of joining a larger group.

Audition

Some ensembles, orchestras, bands, and choirs may require applicants to audition before being invited to join. An audition may include playing one or more prepared songs or sections, sight-reading, playing scales, and improvisation or solo playing. Tips on preparing for auditions are in Chapter 10.

TYPES OF BANDS, ORCHESTRAS, AND OTHER GROUPS

Music can be played with every combination of instruments and musicians you can imagine. There are violists who play with African percussionists, bassoonists who play jazz, opera singers who join rock groups, cellists who play heavy metal, and so on. It goes without saying that there is no clear-cut label for such combos, other than the general terms 'group' or 'ensemble.' Labels for traditional groups aren't exactly standardized or unambiguous either, as you will see on the following pages.

Bands

The word 'band' can refer to a wide variety of musical groups: a four-piece funk group, a school's marching band, a big band (jazz), a one-hundred-piece wind band, or a concert band, for example.

Ensembles

'Ensemble' is another generic term. The word, French for 'together', is often used for classical groups that have five or more members, but are still smaller than an orchestra.

Two to ten

Combinations of two, three, four, or five members are usually called duos, trios, quartets, and quintets respectively; those terms are common in the classical world, but also among jazz musicians, for example. Some also use the labels sextet (six musicians), septet (seven), octet, nonet, or even dectet (ten musicians).

Classification

It's impossible to create a textbook classification for the infinite variety of musical groups, if only because there are so many completely diverse types of groups playing the same style of music, and so many groups with very similar instrumentations playing very different styles of music. Following is a random tour of a number of popular types of ensembles, their instrumentation, and the music they typically play. Please refer to Chapter 9 for short descriptions of the instruments mentioned below.

SCHOOL BANDS AND ORCHESTRAS

In the U.S., some types of ensembles are typically part of school, college, or university music programs, such as concert bands, marching bands, jazz bands, pep bands, and orchestra. Similar groups also exist outside of educational institutions.

Concert bands, symphonic winds
Concert band and symphonic winds are two of the many different names for a large, non-marching group of some forty to more than a hundred woodwind, brasswind, and percussion players. They're also known as wind symphonies, wind bands, wind orchestras, or wind ensembles, their repertoire often including classical music, ballads, musical comedy, jazz, sacred music, patriotic songs, and other styles of music. These ensembles typically incorporate French horns, trumpets, trombones, and other brasswinds, clarinets and saxophones in various voices, flutes and oboes, and orchestral percussion. Other instruments may be added, such as a string section, or a double bass.

Same instrumentation, different level
Some schools have a concert band, a symphonic band, and a wind ensemble, for example. Since each of these groups may have a similar instrumentation and repertoire, their names typically imply either different levels of musicianship or that their members are of different age groups or grades.

Marching band
Marching bands have their roots in the military, and their band members' uniforms typically reflect that heritage. Instead of leading and inspiring the troops, today's marching bands play at sporting events — especially American football games — so they're also referred to as athletic bands. Their repertoire has evolved from marches exclusively to a wide variety of styles, from

pop music to R&B and Christmas songs, arranged for the band's specific instrumentation of woodwinds, brasswinds, and percussion. The woodwinds include a large number of clarinets in various voices, saxophones, flutes, and oboe and bassoon; brasswinds include trumpets and trombones, alto horns, baritones, and tubas; the percussion section uses field drums as well as glockenspiel and other types of pitched percussion instruments. Marching bands also can include stationary instrumentation, such as orchestral timpani and xylophones. These ensembles are often accompanied by so-called 'auxiliaries' such as dancers, color guards, and cheerleaders. If so, they're also known as show bands. A varsity band is a college or university ('varsity') marching band.

Pep bands

A pep band is a subgroup of the marching band. It's a non-marching band that performs at sporting events (basketball, hockey, volleyball, etc.), to rouse team spirit. The repertoire may be comprised of anything from jazz and rock hits to Top 40 and traditional school songs. Pep bands come in any size, from a quartet to a thirty-piece band or an even larger group. The instrumentation includes mostly woodwinds, brasswinds, drums, percussion, and often electric guitar, bass guitar, and keyboards. They're also referred to as stand bands.

Jazz band

Many schools also have a jazz band, which is a stationary band much like a big band or jazz orchestra (see page 178).

More than one

Students often play in more than one group. The pep band may have a lot of the same faces that you'll see in the marching band or the jazz band, for example.

Orchestra

Most (beginning) school orchestras consist of string players only. Orchestras play more than classical music. Their repertoire often includes popular music, television and movie themes, Broadway favorites, and so on. The full orchestra is made up of members of both the band (wind and percussion) and the orchestra.

CHAPTER 8

Strolling strings
Strolling strings are an alternative to the traditional orchestra. The string players don't march, but stroll through the crowd at community events, banquets, art shows, and other functions, playing various types of popular music.

MORE BANDS

There are many types of uniformed marching and non-marching bands outside of the educational world. Some examples?

Drum corps
Drum and bugle corps, or drum corps for short, are typically competitive efforts. Their competitions take place on football fields, the highly stylized performances lasting some ten to twelve minutes each. Traditionally, corps use brasswinds in the key of G only, commonly referred to as soprano bugles, alto bugles (such as mellophones), tenor bugles (baritone, euphonium), and bass bugles. Today, they may also use brasswinds in other keys. In addition to field drums, these bands also use pit percussion, such as xylophones, marimbas, or timpani. Color guards, flags, rifles, or sabers are an important element of the corps. Drum corps members can be almost any age, from under seven to over sixty-five. Drums corps are regulated by organizations such as Drum Corps International (DCI), Drum Corps Associates (DCA), and DCUK.

Parade bands
There are different types of parade bands, which usually feature a combination of drums and other instruments such as bagpipes or fifes. Ancient fife and drum corps use keyed and keyless transverse flutes (fifes) and traditional rope-tensioned drums.

Brass bands
Brass bands, comprised of brasswinds and percussion instruments, have British roots. The British (short) cornet is the

PLAYING TOGETHER

brass band's leading voice. Most of the brass instruments used, including flugelhorns, euphoniums, baritones, and tubas feature a conical bore: The instruments gradually becoming wider from the mouthpiece towards the bell. This makes for the characteristic warm, sweet, or mellow sound of this type of band. The repertoire may include marches, traditionals, folk songs, hymns, rags, and classical transcriptions, but also jazz and pop songs.

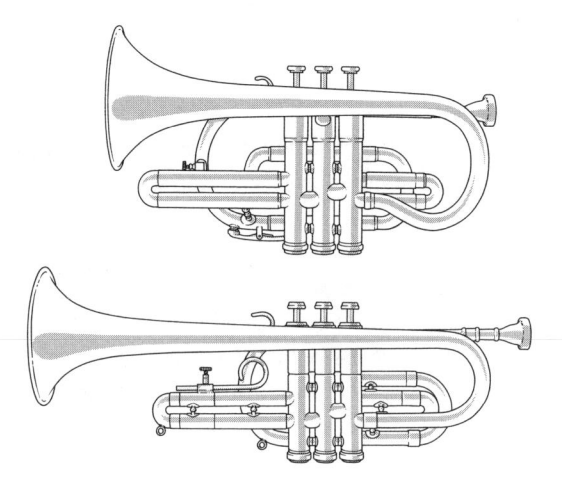

British (upper) and American cornets.

Scramble bands
Some 'marching' bands do not necessarily march. Scramble bands, for example, use an instrumentation that is a hodgepodge of everything from cellos and accordions to harps and bass guitar. Even non-musicians can join in with pots and pans — literally.

CLASSICAL MUSIC

Classical music is played by a variety of groups and ensembles dedicated strictly to the genre. The largest type of group is the symphony orchestra. (A symphony is a composition that typically consists of four large parts or movements.) Symphony orchestras usually have between fifty and more than a hundred members, with the majority of them playing strings. In large orchestras,

CHAPTER 8

there can be more than sixty string players (e.g., sixteen first violinists, fourteen second violinists, twelve violists, ten cellists and eight double bassists) in addition to sixteen woodwind players (flutes, clarinets, oboes, bassoons), sixteen brasswinds (trumpets, trombones, French horns, tuba), three to four percussionists, one or two timpanists, two harpists, and a pianist. Other instruments may be included as well, such as a saxophone, though many famous symphonies were written before the birth of this instrument, around 1840.

Philharmonic orchestra
Some symphony orchestras are known as philharmonic orchestras. 'Philharmonic' literally translates as 'music-loving,' while the word 'symphony' basically means 'sounding (well) together.'

Chamber orchestra
A chamber orchestra is a similar type of ensemble, yet smaller. The number of string players typically varies from twenty to thirty, and there are two rather than four players for most wind instruments. There are even smaller chamber orchestras as well.

Ensemble
The term 'ensemble' commonly implies a group featuring one instrumentalist for each musical part. In an orchestra, there is always more than one string player playing each part.

Chamber ensembles
Chamber ensembles are typically subcategorized according to the primary featured instrument(s) and the number of players, such as the following examples:

- **String quartet**s: two violins, one viola, one cello

- **String quintets**: two violins, two violas, one cello; or two violins, one viola, two cellos

- **Wind trios**: one clarinet, one bassoon, one French horn

- **Wind quintets**: one clarinet, one bassoon, one French horn, one oboe, one flute

- **Brass quintets**: two trumpets, one French horn, one trombone, one tuba or bass trombone
- **Piano trio**: one piano, one violin, one cello

Non-standard
Next to numerous compositions for such standard ensembles, there are many works for nonstandard groups: trumpet and vocal, or three brasswinds and piano, and so on. Also, music written for one type of ensemble can be arranged for different instruments, e.g., string quartets can be rewritten for four saxophonists. *Tip:* The term 'string quartet' can refer to both the ensemble itself and to a work for that type of ensemble.

Contemporary music
There is no standard instrumentation for ensembles that play contemporary classical music written by twentieth and twenty-first century composers. These compositions may include arrangements for everything from electronic instruments to violins, anvils, horns, and radios.

THE SAME INSTRUMENT

A clarinet choir features most or all of the clarinet voices, from the small, high-pitched A♭ sopranino clarinet to the large, low-pitched bass clarinet. Similar ensembles exist for other instrumentalists at all levels, from amateur to professional: There are saxophone choirs, flute orchestras, accordion ensembles, and so on. Some of these groups include a rhythm section (piano, bass, drums) or other instruments. The term 'orchestra' is usually reserved for the largest of these groups, typically with fifty or more musicians. Repertoires can range from classical pieces to marches, international folk music, pop songs, and arrangements of compositions for concert bands and symphony orchestras.

CHAPTER 8

VOCAL GROUPS

In a vocal group, all members 'play' the same instrument: the singing voice. The term choir is often used for religious vocal groups that sing sacred music or gospel songs, but there are secular groups that are called choirs as well. Other generic names for vocal groups are chorus, chorale, or choral ensemble. Small vocal groups also use the labels trio, quartet, and so on.

School choirs
Schools often have more than one choir. Some are open to all interested students, others require singing experience, an audition, or both.

Easy access
There are many vocal groups (boy, girl, or mixed) that your child can join without any previous experience, ranging from community choirs to church choirs. Their repertoires can vary from hymns to rock songs.

More
Joining a choir provides children with the opportunity to develop their voices, learn to sing and breathe correctly, work on their stage performance, etc. The amount of guidance provided to choir members regarding their vocal and musical development may differ per choir, of course: Some choirs sing just for fun; others have strong educational elements.

GUITARS, BASS, DRUMS, AND MORE

With one or two guitars, a bass guitar, and a drum set, you can play the entire history of rock and roll and numerous more-or-less closely related styles — soul, gospel, country, R&B, funk, and so on.

PLAYING TOGETHER

Four elements
The typical rock band's instrumentation perfectly demonstrates the four major elements of this and many other types of music. The drummer provides the element of rhythm, in close cooperation with the bassist, who of course plays the bass part. This duo is responsible for the music's foundation, so to speak. The vocalist or the solo guitarist provides the melody, while the second guitarist (a.k.a. the rhythm guitar player) plays chords, providing the element of harmony to the music.

More instruments
Many bands use additional musicians, such as one or more keyboard players, a percussionist (coloring the music with congas, timbales, bells, cymbals, and so on), one or more horn players (trumpet, trombone, saxophone), or backing vocalists. The acoustic steel-string guitar is often used next to an electric guitar. Some bands use less traditional instruments such as the (electric) violin, the flute, or a tuba. The turntable, played by a DJ, has found its place within quite a few bands as well (see page 208).

Guitars come in all kinds of styles and shapes.

TIPBOOK MUSIC FOR KIDS AND TEENS

CHAPTER 8

JAZZ

Jazz is a term that describes an enormous array of musical styles, and there are jazz ensembles with all sorts of line-ups. Basically, a jazz trio consists of a drummer, a bassist, and a pianist or a guitarist. In a quartet, the fourth musician typically is a horn player (saxophone or trumpet, for example); in a quintet, a second horn player is added to the basic line-up.

Big band
A big band, a.k.a. swing band, dance band or jazz orchestra traditionally plays music from the 1930s and 1940s (the so-called swing era), but there are big bands that play contemporary or latin-oriented music too. A typical big band has the same basis as smaller jazz groups, i.e. drums, bass, and piano. This so-called rhythm section can be extended with a guitarist or a percussionist, for example. The other musicians play wind instruments: some three to five trumpets, the same number of trombones, two alto and two tenor saxophones, and a baritone saxophone. Clarinet, flute, and other instruments may be included as well.

Dixieland
Some types of jazz bands have very typical line-ups. In a Dixieland band, for example, you'll likely find a tuba rather than a double bass, a clarinet rather than a saxophone, a cornet rather than a trumpet, and a banjo rather than a guitar.

Today and tomorrow
In today's jazz, any combination of instruments can be found onstage. A trio of electric cello, piano, and tuba? No problem.

Fusion
Jazz has often been merged with other styles of music, from latin to classical music, and from rock to traditional music from India. The possibilities are endless. So-called fusion bands often feature electric bass guitar, drums, keyboards (piano or electronic keyboard instruments), electric guitar, and one or more horns, for example.

PLAYING TOGETHER

Instruments

Electric guitars come in many different guises. On page 177, two extremes are shown. Likewise, a jazz drum set is quite different from the kit a symphonic-rock drummer may use, the latter typically consisting of drums and cymbals in larger numbers and sizes.

A large rock drum set, and a small jazz kit.

AND MORE

There are many more types of bands, which are often correlated to specific styles, and some use very specific instruments. Again, some random examples:

- In a **bluegrass** band, you'll find guitars, a double bass, a fiddle (a violin that's played and possibly tuned differently), a five-string banjo, and a mandolin.

CHAPTER 8

A five-string banjo.

- A **klezmer band** plays Jewish folk music. The violin and clarinet are important voices that are often accompanied by another violin (playing rhythmic patterns, just like in traditional gypsy music), as well as an accordion, drums (bass drum, snare drum, cymbals), and a brasswind bass instrument.

- A typical **salsa** band, playing what could be described as New York Latin music, has no less than three percussionists (playing bongos, congas, and timbales), a bassist, a pianist, one or more singers, and horns (trumpet, trombone, saxophones and/or flute).

cowbells

congas

timbales

TIPBOOK MUSIC FOR KIDS AND TEENS

- The Mexican **mariachi** combines standard instruments such as the violin, trumpet, and acoustic guitar with typical Mexican instruments such as the vihuela (a small, round-backed five-string guitar), a Mexican harp, and the guitarron (a large guitar-like instrument that plays the bass part).

- And then there are more than enough small and large groups playing **non-Western** music to fill another series of Tipbooks. Most non-Western cultures have their own musical styles and instruments.

9

The Instruments

Though you're probably familiar with many of the instruments mentioned in this book, the information in the following chapter may give you a better understanding of the differences between families of instruments, as well as of the instruments themselves. Most importantly, this chapter focuses on instruments accessible to beginning players. For more detailed information, please refer to the Tipbook on your instrument, or other instrument-specific resources.

CHAPTER 9

Classifying instruments is just as difficult as classifying bands and orchestras. Some examples.

- The violin, the viola, the cello and the double bass are **orchestral string instruments**, but they're also frequently used outside of orchestras.

- The same instruments are also known as **bowed instruments** because they're played with a bow — but the strings of the double bass are often plucked instead.

- The bass guitar belongs to the family of **fretted string instruments**, but many bassists play fretless bass guitars (see the next paragraph).

- The term **strings** is often used to indicate the orchestral strings, but technically covers all string instruments, including the piano.

- The piano can be seen as **a percussion instrument** (the hammers hit the piano strings much like a drummer hits the drum heads), but it also qualifies as **a string instrument** (it has more strings than any other instrument!). This book classifies it as a **keyboard instrument**.

STRING INSTRUMENTS

The family of string instruments (a.k.a stringed instruments) has two main subgroups: the orchestral strings, or simply 'strings,' and the fretted string instruments such as the guitar. Unlike orchestral string instruments, guitars and bass guitars have small metal bars (frets) on the fingerboard. Frets make playing in tune easier: It is the exact position of the fret that produces the exact pitch of the note you play, rather than the exact position of your finger. So why don't violins have frets? Because they'd make the instrument sound quite different. Likewise, fretless bass guitars don't sound the same as the standard fretted version, and you don't need to be an expert to hear the difference.

THE INSTRUMENTS

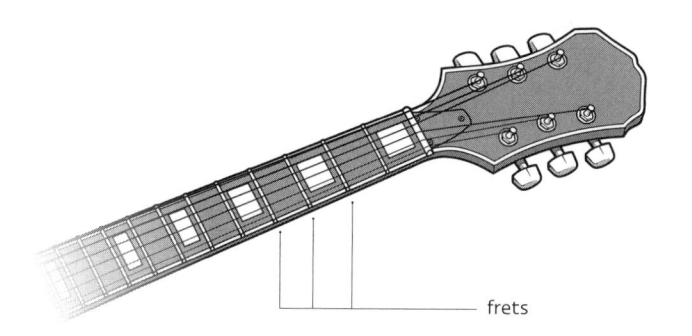

The frets on a steel-string guitar.

frets

Orchestral string instruments

The violin is the most widely played orchestral string instrument. It's used in numerous musical styles, from classical to gypsy jazz to country. The viola is slightly larger, which makes it sound a little lower and 'warmer'. Its highest three strings sound the same pitch as the lowest three violin strings (G, D, A), and its fourth string sounds a lower C. The cello is considerably larger yet. Its four strings are tuned to the same notes as viola strings, only an octave lower (C, G, D, A). The cello and the viola are not often found outside of classical circles, but there's no reason why they shouldn't be. Some musicians even use these instruments to play heavy metal!

Tipcode KIDS-005, KIDS-006, KIDS-007

Tipcode KIDS-005 demonstrates the difference between a violin and a viola; Tipcodes KIDS-006 and 007 briefly display the versatility of the violin and the cello respectively.

TIPCODE

Double bass

The double bass (a.k.a. upright bass, string bass) looks like the big brother of the other three, but it's actually more of a distant cousin. It typically features sloped shoulders and a flat back, rather

185

TIPBOOK MUSIC FOR KIDS AND TEENS

CHAPTER 9

than an arched one. The tuning is different as well. Bass strings are a fourth apart rather than a fifth, and tuned to E, A, D, G, from low to high. Another difference is that a double bass has metal tuning machines, rather than the wooden tuning pegs of a violin or cello. This instrument is frequently used outside of the classical realm (mainly in jazz), in which case it is usually plucked instead of bowed. A bass guitar uses the same tuning.

TIPCODE

Tipcode KIDS-008
The double bass can be played with a bow (con arco) or plucked (pizzicato).

Guitars

The guitar comes in many sizes and shapes. First of all, there are acoustic and electric guitars. Electric guitars require an amplifier, while the feeble sound of the strings of an acoustic guitar is amplified acoustically by the large, hollow sound box of the instrument.

Acoustic guitars

There are two basic types of acoustic guitars: those with nylon strings, and those with steel strings. They look similar at first sight, but their bodies feature different shapes and sizes, their heads (at the very end of the neck) are different, and steel-string guitars have a narrower neck. Nylon-string guitars or Spanish guitars are mostly used for classical music, but it finds it way into other styles of music as well, from folk to jazz. The steel-string guitar has a brighter, slightly louder sound that lends itself better to pop, country, or folk music. Steel-string guitars are available in various models, from the large Jumbo and Dreadnought guitars to the small Concert guitar.

THE INSTRUMENTS

Classical, Spanish, or nylon-string guitar.

Steel-string, western, or folk guitar.

Tipcode KIDS-009
To hear the difference between a nylon-string and a steel-string acoustic guitar, play this Tipcode.

Variations
There are many variations on the acoustic guitar, such as:

- **Acoustic-electrics**: acoustic guitars with a built-in pickup, allowing you to plug it into an (acoustic) guitar amplifier. Such guitars usually feature an onboard preamplifier with volume and tone controls, as well as some effects or a tuner, for example.

The control panel of an acoustic-electric guitar.

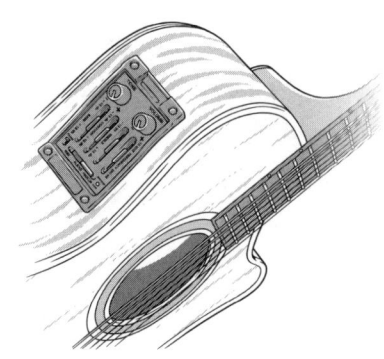

- **Resonator guitars**: instruments with a wooden or metal top with built-in resonators that amplify the sound and give it a very specific character.
- **Flamenco guitars** and other types of guitars that have been designed with a certain style of music or type of playing in mind.

Electric guitars

The most popular electric guitar designs haven't changed much since their introduction in the early 1950s. Most electric guitars have a solid body rather than the hollow, resonating sound box with a vibrating top that characterizes the acoustic guitar. This solid body is the reason that electric guitars hardly make any sound without an amplifier (which makes them great for silent practice!). The sound of the instrument is produced through one, two, or three pickups that literally 'pick up' the vibrations of the strings and convert them to electrical signals. These signals are sent to an amplifier, which boosts them and sends them to a speaker.

Different types

There are many types of electric guitars, many of them designed for a certain style of music (country, hard rock, metal, blues, and so on), while others can be found on a wide variety of stages. Jazz players typically use a particular type of electric guitar that

THE INSTRUMENTS

features a hollow body with an arched top, and two f-holes, just like a violin (see page 177).

Gibson Les Paul®.

Fender Stratocaster®.

Tipcode KIDS-010
Electric guitarists often use effects, such as a wah-wah, a chorus, or a delay.

Bass guitar
The bass guitar, also introduced in the early 1950s, has the same type of body and neck as an electric guitar and the same tuning as a double bass. Next to the traditional four-string model, there are bass guitars with five, six, and even more strings. Fretless bass guitars have become quite common as well. They're mostly used by advanced players, who like them for their specific tone.

189

TIPBOOK MUSIC FOR KIDS AND TEENS

CHAPTER 9

TIPCODE

Tipcode KIDS-011
Here you can hear a few examples of how you can influence the sound of a bass guitar sound by using the tone control on the bass amplifier and applying some different, basic playing techniques.

Electric violins
Guitars and basses are not the only stringed instruments that come in electric versions. There are electric violins (with or without frets, and with four or more strings), and a few companies make electric cellos and upright basses. Some electric violins and cellos are specifically designed for silent practice, as shown on page 92.

Harp
The harp is played by plucking the strings, typically with eight fingers. Most harps have 26 to 28 strings, while the professional pedal harp has 47 strings. To be able to play music in various keys, you need to adjust the pitch of a number of those strings. On a lever harp, you do so by adjusting a number of levers. The pedal harp has a set of pedals that allow you to adjust the pitch of all relevant strings in one move. Pedal harps are expensive instruments, prices typically starting around fifteen thousand dollars. Next to a huge collection of classical music, there is also folk and pop music for the harp.

Mandolin.

Mandolin
The original mandolin is clearly related to the lute. Today's mandolins, however, look quite different. They still have a short neck, but they typically feature an arched top and a flat back. A mandolin has four pairs of strings. The strings of each each pair or *course* are tuned in unison (i.e., to the same pitch).

Banjo
The banjo (see page 180) has a round body with a plastic 'skin' for a top, just like a drum. It has four or five strings and a very short, percussive sound, and is usually played with finger picks. Five-string banjos are mainly used in bluegrass and country. The four-string version is often played in folk and Dixieland bands.

Dulcimer
The strings of the hammered dulcimer are played using mallet hammers, typically made of wood. The instrument is mainly used to play folk music. Like the mandolin, most dulcimers have strings in unison pairs.

Saz, bouzouki, balalaika
Most cultures have their own string instruments. One example is the Turkish saz-baglama, more commonly known as the saz, with adjustable frets, a long neck, and a relatively small body. Others include the somewhat similar-looking Greek bouzouki; the long-necked Russian balalaika, with its triangular body; and the Bulgarian tambura, with a very shallow, pear-shaped body and four pairs of strings. The list is virtually endless.

WOODWINDS

The recorder is one of the most basic woodwind instruments. All its family members work along the same principle. If you play the instrument, you make the air column inside the instrument's body vibrate, and vibrating air is sound.

CHAPTER 9

Toneholes
Like most other woodwind instruments, the recorder has a series of toneholes in its body. Opening and closing those toneholes changes the effective length of the body, and thus the length of the air column, which makes for a different pitch. When all toneholes are closed, the air column is at its maximum length, and the recorder will produce its lowest note. With each tonehole you open, from the lowest one up, the air column gets shorter and a higher note will sound.

Non-wood woodwinds
As you will see below, woodwind instruments aren't necessarily made of wood: Saxophones are made of brass, most flutes have a metal body, and many student clarinets, oboes, and piccolos have a plastic body.

Plastic
Student oboes and clarinets are often plastic instruments. This makes them less vulnerable for cracking than wooden models. They also need less care and maintenance, and they're weather resistant. Wooden instruments usually produce a warmer, darker tone. This is not because they're made of wood per se, but because they're typically better-constructed, higher-quality (and thus more expensive) instruments than the plastic student models.

Flute
The flute is a transverse or side-blown instrument with a number of keys that cover the toneholes. Original flutes were made of wood. Nowadays, most flute players opt for a metal instrument. Just about all student flutes are silver-plated. The more money you spend on an instrument, the more parts will be made of solid silver. This material enhances both the instrument's sound and its longevity. The piccolo is a smaller, higher-pitched flute with a metal or wooden body, or plastic for some student models. There are also lower-pitched flutes such as the alto flute and the rare bass flute.

Clarinet
The clarinet has the same type of keys as a flute. The body is usually made of plastic (for student instruments) or wood, but

THE INSTRUMENTS

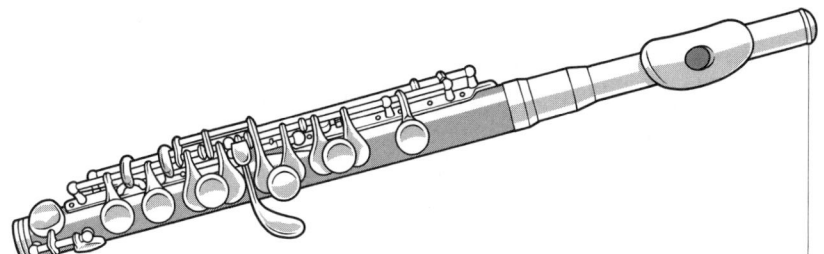

The piccolo, a small and high-pitched flute.

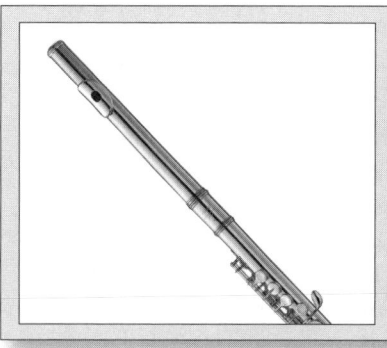

Tipcodes KIDS-012, KIDS-013
In Tipcodes KIDS-012 and KIDS-013 you can hear the sound of a flute and a piccolo respectively.

TIPCODE

there are metal clarinets as well. A major difference between the flute and the clarinet is in the way the sound is generated: The clarinet has a mouthpiece with a single piece of cane — the reed — attached to it. When you play the instrument, the reed vibrates, which makes the air inside the instrument vibrate. The main clarinet voice is the B♭ clarinet. Other popular voices are the higher-pitched E♭ clarinet, and the lower sounding A, alto, and bass clarinets.

Tipcode KIDS-014
This Tipcode once again plays the ranges of the four main clarinet voices. The third one, The B♭ clarinet is the most popular voice.

TIPCODE

193

TIPBOOK MUSIC FOR KIDS AND TEENS

CHAPTER 9

TIP

Attractive names
Because the word 'plastic' may sound a bit cheap, most manufacturers come up with a more attractive name for the material they use, such as Resotone, Resonite, Sonority Resin, or Grena 2000. Plastic clarinets are also referred to as composite, resin, or synthetic clarinets.

Saxophone
The saxophone has a similar key mechanism and mouthpiece: Both the clarinet and the saxophone are single-reed instruments. The major difference is that the clarinet has a largely cylindrical body, while the saxophone has a conical body, getting steadily wider from the mouthpiece onwards. This makes the instrument sound and play quite differently. Alto and tenor saxophones are the most widely used voices, followed by the larger baritone saxophone and the smaller soprano. Even though saxophones are made of brass, they do belong to the woodwind family.

TIPCODE

Tipcodes KIDS-015, KIDS-016, KIDS-017, KIDS-018
These four Tipcodes demonstrate the different tones of the soprano, the alto, the tenor, and the baritone saxophone, starting with the soprano.

Oboe and bassoon
The oboe and the bassoon are also reed instruments, but they each feature a double reed, i.e., a double piece of cane. The oboe has a conical body, like the saxophone. Student models are made of plastic, while professional models are made of wood. The bassoon is a large and expensive instrument with a body that consists of two wooden (or plastic) 'tubes.' The reed is attached to the bocal, a curved metal tube. Players usually support the instrument

THE INSTRUMENTS

with a seat strap, a neck strap, or a special type of support. The contrabassoon is a lower-pitched version of the bassoon. The English horn, another double-reed instrument, is the only woodwind that's officially known as a 'horn'.

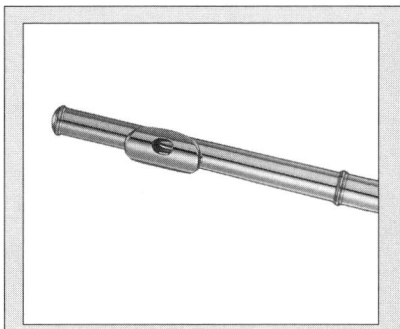

Tipcode KIDS-019
The characteristic sound of the oboe and the intriguing tone of the bassoon can be heard here.

TIPCODE

Panflute
The panflute is an example of a woodwind instrument that has no toneholes. Instead, it consists of a series of individual flutes, each flute producing a specific pitch.

BRASSWINDS

Brasswinds do not have a vibrating reed. Instead, they're played by vibrating (or 'buzzing') your lips in the instrument's mouthpiece. Larger brasswinds have larger mouthpieces. The buzzing lips are sometimes referred to as the lip reed, and some call brasswinds lip-reed instruments.

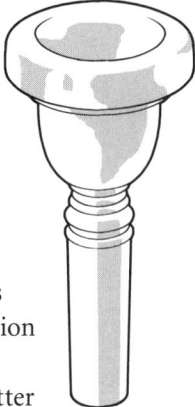

A trumpet mouthpiece.

Different pitches
On brasswinds, you play notes of different pitches using your embouchure (simply put: your lip tension and the way you blow the instrument) and by varying the total length of the instrument. The latter

CHAPTER 9

is most visible on a trombone. Extending the slide makes the tube of the instrument longer. A trombone slide has seven positions, making for seven different tube lengths. In each position, you can play a series of different pitches.

Trumpets
Most trumpets have three valves. Pressing a valve makes the tube of the instrument (and thus the vibrating air column) a bit longer. The three valves make for seven different tube lengths, just like the slide of the trombone. And again, you can play a series of different pitches with each valve combination. Most other brasswind instruments have three or four valves.

Conical instruments
Trumpets are a bit harder to blow and they sound brighter than most other brasswinds. This is because the tube or body of a trumpet is much less conical than that of other brasswinds, offering more resistance. If you compare a trumpet to a flugelhorn, for example, you will see that the latter is much wider at the end. This stronger flare makes the flugelhorn easier to blow, and it generates a much warmer, mellower sound.

The flugelhorn (below) has a much stronger flare than the trumpet (above): It is just as wide at the mouthpiece, but much wider at the bell.

Cornet
There are two basic types of cornet: the British or European model, and the American cornet. The latter looks much longer,

THE INSTRUMENTS

Tipcode KIDS-020
Here you will hear the difference between a trumpet and a bugle, first played by a classically trained musician, then by a jazz trumpeter.

TIPCODE

but the length of their tubing is identical. The American cornet is more like the trumpet, whereas the British cornet or short cornet is more like the flugelhorn. Both instruments are shown on page 173.

French horn

The French horn, with its circular tubing, looks very different from other brasswinds. It has a very different timbre as well, and its mouthpiece is small compared to that of other brasswinds. Another difference is the active role of the player's right hand: Moving it within the bell of the instrument controls the timbre and the exact pitch of the notes.

Low brass

Most brass instruments listed above are categorized as soprano or treble (high-pitched) brasswinds. Likewise, the lower-pitched brasswinds are collectively known as low brass.

Background brass

Many low brass instruments also belong to the category of background brasswinds: They're typically used 'in the background' as an accompaniment for other (brass) instruments. Still, the tuba and all other background instruments can be used for soloing as well.

Tuba

The word 'tuba' commonly refers to the bass tuba, which has a tube around twenty-five feet (!) long. Bass tubas come in C, for symphony orchestras, and in B♭, for brass bands, concert bands, and other wind ensembles. Tubas pitched in F and E♭ are one size smaller. The low pitches of the tuba are typically indicated as CC ('double C'), BB♭ ('double B-flat'), FF, and EE♭.

Saxhorns
Around 1845, when Adolph Sax was still perfecting his saxophone, he was granted a patent on a whole family of saxhorns, from large to small. Some of those instruments are still in use, such as the tenor horn and the baritone. The baritone is very similar to the euphonium, but a euphonium has a wider bore and a larger bell. As a result, it sounds somewhat bigger and warmer. The two lowest-sounding saxhorns are pretty much the same instruments as the large B♭ and E♭ tubas.

Confusing
Many brass instruments have different names in different countries. For example, the tenor tuna, an instrument that sounds an octave higher than the regular bass tuba, is known as a euphonium in some countries, and as a bass tuba (!) or alto horn in other areas.

Marching brasswinds
Regular tubas, horns, and trombones are tricky to play while marching, so the industry has come up with various alternative instruments. A well-known example is the sousaphone. This 'circular tuba' has an enormous forward-facing bell, often made of a lighter, synthetic material to save weight. This instrument is also used in dixieland bands, for example. The opening of the bell is sometimes covered with an acoustically transparent cloth that states the name of the band, much like the resonant head on a bass drum in a rock group.

On your shoulder
You can also get trumpet-shaped euphoniums, tubas, and other brass instruments designed so you can rest them on your left shoulder, making them easier to march with. The bells of these instruments point forwards instead of upwards, so the sound is projected toward the audience. Some companies make convertible instruments, such as an upright tuba that can be converted to a marching instrument – and back.

THE INSTRUMENTS

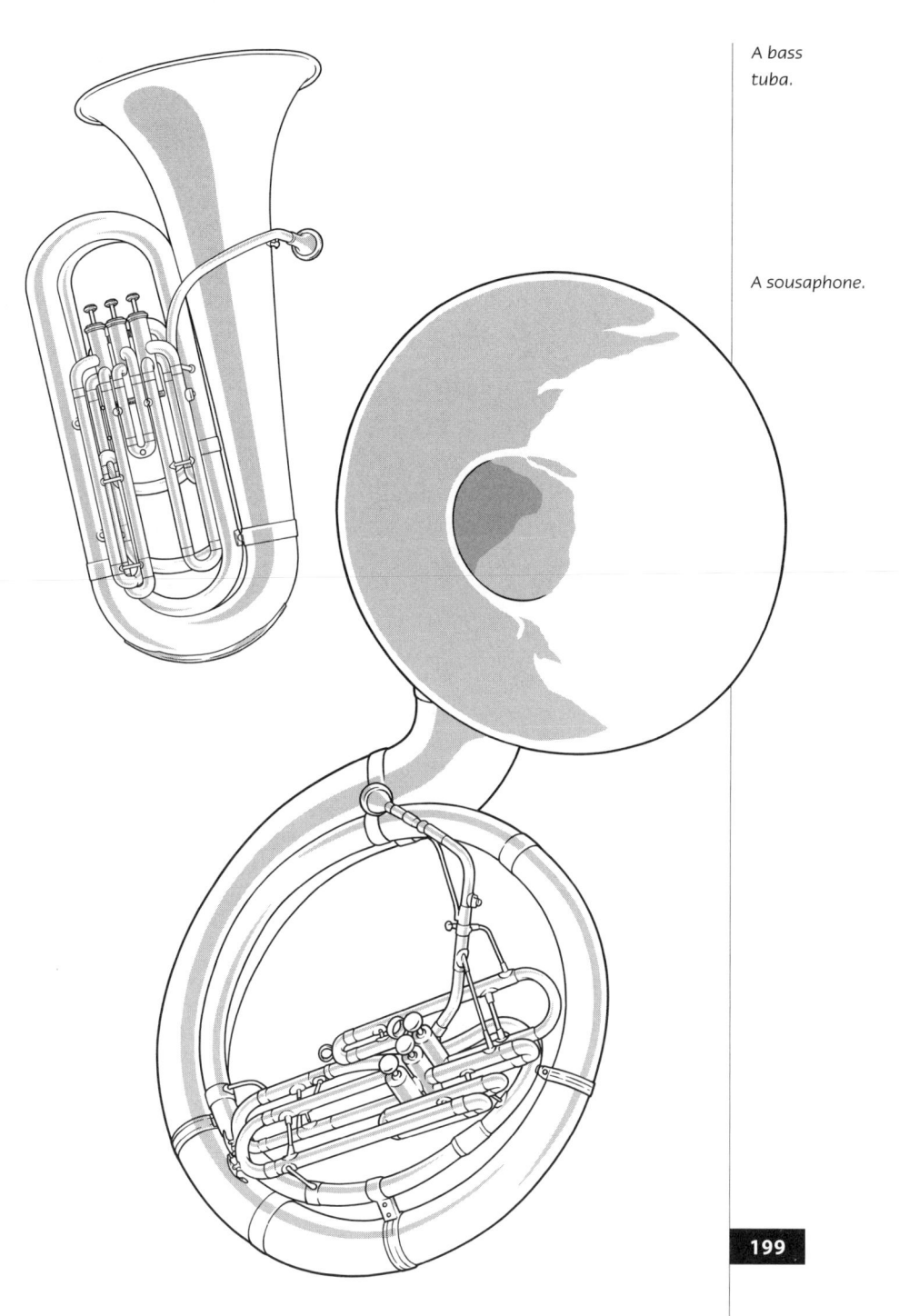

A bass tuba.

A sousaphone.

199

TIPBOOK MUSIC FOR KIDS AND TEENS

CHAPTER 9

Without valves
Brass instruments without valves are referred to as natural instruments. Some examples are the natural trumpet or clarion, the hunting horn, and the bugle. These instruments can produce a limited number of (natural) pitches only.

KEYBOARD INSTRUMENTS

The one thing all keyboard instruments have in common is, of course, the keyboard. Though that keyboard can make them look a lot alike at first glance, each type of keyboard instrument requires a different playing technique. Pianists, for example, control the volume of their notes mainly with their keys, while organ players can't: their instruments are not touch sensitive. And while an organ continues to produce sound as long as you hold a key down, a piano tone will slowly fade away.

Piano
The piano is often considered the world's most versatile acoustic instrument. It sounds notes lower than a bass and higher than a piccolo; you can play chords, bass lines, and melodies on it, all at the same time. It can be used in almost any style of music, all by itself, to accompany a choir, or as a solo instrument with a large orchestra, and so on. It's also the favorite instrument of many composers, and a great secondary instrument for any

TIPCODE

Tipcode KIDS-021
This Tipcode clearly demonstrates the versatility of the piano, as well as the fact that the instrument is often considered an orchestra on its own.

musician, if only because the layout of the keyboard makes many musical concepts (scales, chords, intervals, etc.) so much easier to understand.

Digital piano

A digital piano doesn't have strings. Instead, it typically uses samples: digital recordings of piano (and other) sounds. The specific feel of a piano keyboard, caused by the complicated mechanism that makes the hammers hit the strings, is mimicked on most digital pianos. This feature is known as a hammer action keyboard or weighted action keyboard, for example.

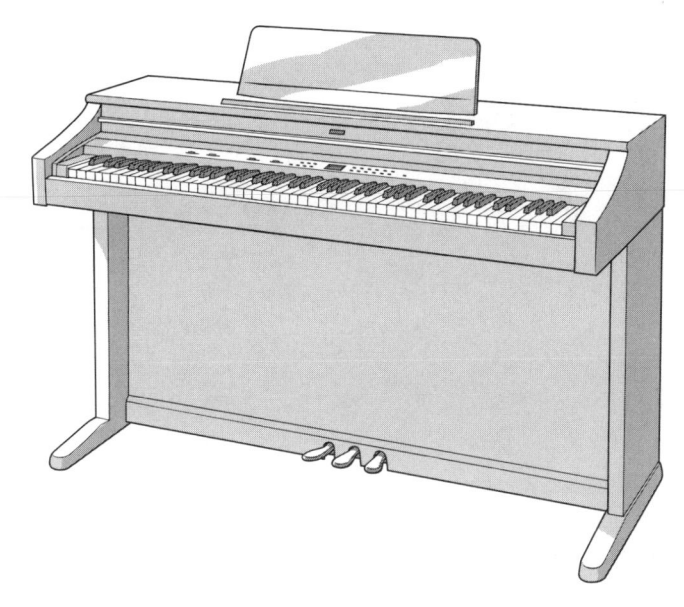

A basic digital piano with a weighted action.

A different instrument

Even though today's digital piano sounds and feels really close to the acoustic instrument, most pianists still find it a different instrument. This has much to do with the fact that the sound is produced by speakers rather than by the large wooden sound board that characterizes the traditional piano sound. The main advantages of digital pianos are that they cost less, they require virtually no maintenance, they weigh much less, they can be played with headphones, they usually come equipped with a built-in sequencer to record what you play, and they have many

CHAPTER 9

additional features (various sounds, effects, and so on). On the other hand, acoustic pianos last much longer, they have a higher resale value, and they provide you with the true, rich sound and feel of the instrument.

Hybrid piano
A hybrid piano offers the best of both worlds. It's an acoustic piano equipped with a built-in digital piano. If silent practice is required, a pedal- or lever-operated rail stops the hammers from hitting the strings while a small digital sound module provides the sampled piano sounds, or any other sounds available, from strings to vibraphone. This device is usually located under the keyboard, as shown below.

A sound module with extensive options.

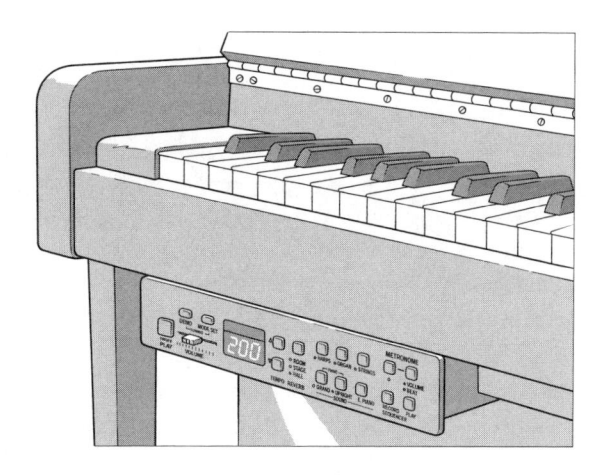

Home keyboard
A home keyboard is an easily accessible instrument featuring numerous built-in sounds (samples, again), ranging from saxophones and flutes to electric guitars, synthesized sounds, percussion, strings, handclaps, birds, and a variety of sound effects. Piano sounds are also included, but most home keyboards don't sound as natural as digital pianos, and they don't have a piano-type (hammer action) keyboard. One of the main features of a home keyboard is the accompaniment section. This built-in virtual ensemble supplements your playing with piano or guitar chords, a bass part, drums and percussion, strings, horns, and so on: Home keyboards are true one-man orchestras.

THE INSTRUMENTS

Organ
Today's electronic organs and home keyboards are very similarly equipped, with a few exceptions: Organs have a larger number of organ sounds, of course; they typically come with bass pedals, and they have a volume pedal and twin keyboards. There are non-electronic organs as well, such as the traditional church organs.

Synthesizer
While a home keyboard basically has preset sounds and an accompaniment section, a synthesizer allows you to create (synthesize) completely original sounds. These instruments provide you with samples or electronically generated tones and a wide range of electronic filters, allowing you to mold sounds into almost any aural shape you like. The difference between home keyboards, synths, and other electronic keyboard instruments (e.g., samplers, workstations, groove machines) isn't always really clear, as there is a growing number of common features. Synthesizers are not typically chosen by beginning musicians.

Accordion
The accordion is another keyboard instrument. You might see it as a wind instrument too: Its tone is produced by vibrating metal reeds, much like the reeds in harmonicas or mouth harps. The right hand plays the melody, operating either a button keyboard (a.k.a. chromatic keyboard) or a keyboard with a standard piano-type layout. The left hand plays the chords, operating a button keyboard where each single button triggers a chord, while it also operates the bellows, moving air through the instrument.

DRUMS AND PERCUSSION

The family of drums and percussion instruments is probably the largest family of musical instruments, comprising basically everything that produces a sound when hit or shaken. Drum set players usually play drum kit only, and the timpani in a symphony orchestra are played by a dedicated timpanist. Many other

CHAPTER 9

drummers and percussionists play a whole range of instruments. For percussion students, this includes the snare drum, the bass drum and other drums, cymbals, one or more mallet instruments, and other instruments. Percussionists in (pop, fusion, Latin, etc.) bands usually play a large variety of instruments, from congas, bongos and timbales, to bells, shakers, and an infinite collection of related gear.

Drums

There are three types of drums found in marching bands, concert bands, and symphony orchestras — snare, bass, and toms — and it's these same three drums that form the basis of a drum set. In each type of band, these drums may have different dimensions and tunings, but their main characteristics are the same:

- The **snare drum** produces a crisp, articulate sound. Its heads are tuned quite high. The characteristic 'crisp' sound is produced by a set of (wire) snares under the lower head.
- The **bass drum** sounds like its name suggests, providing the heart beat in a large variety of musical styles.
- A series of **toms** in different sizes, producing different pitches, provide the melodic element in the drum section.

Field drums

Marching drummers typically use deep-shelled snare drums, relatively shallow bass drums, and single-headed toms known as tenor drums, multi-tenors, or timp toms. The specific types of drums used by marching drummers are known as field drums, and they're sometimes referred to as marching drums.

Orchestral drums

Orchestral drummers use a shallower type of snare drum. Their bass drum is usually much bigger (it doesn't need to be carried around!). The single-headed toms are called concert toms.

Drum set

In a drum set, all featured drums are played by a single drummer. The snare drum stands between the drummer's knees, while the bass drum is played with a pedal-operated beater. In a standard

THE INSTRUMENTS

five-piece setup, two small, double-headed toms are mounted on the bass drum (mounted toms or rack toms). A third tom, the larger and thus lower-pitched floor tom, traditionally has its own three legs. Mounted floor toms are also used.

A standard five-piece drum set.

Tipcode KIDS-022
This brief video shows you the different components of a basic, five-piece drum set.

TIPCODE

Cymbals
A set drummer also uses a number of cymbals in different sizes and thicknesses. Among them are the hi-hat cymbals. This cymbal

205

TIPBOOK MUSIC FOR KIDS AND TEENS

pair is played with another pedal, the hi-hat pedal. Marching and orchestral drummers often use cymbal pairs too, striking one against the other.

Timpani

Timpani are a very different type of drums. They produce a clearly identifiable pitch (they're tuned to specific notes, unlike most other drums), and they have a kettle instead of a cylindrical shell. Timpani are used in orchestras and pit percussion sections.

Melodic percussion

Melodic percussion instruments have metal or wooden keys arranged in a way similar to the piano keyboard. The fact that they're played with mallets explains their other name, mallet instruments.

- A **glockenspiel** has a series of small metal keys, producing a piercing, bell-like sound. Orchestral glockenspiels are also known as orchestral bells.

- **Xylophones**, used in both marching and orchestral settings, have narrow wooden or plastic keys with small resonators.

- A **marimba** has wider, larger wooden keys with large resonators, making for a much warmer tone.

- The **vibraphone** is mainly used in jazz bands. Its wide metal keys have resonators with rotating metal discs that make the instrument's sound 'vibrate'.

- The **steel drum** is a different type of instrument. Technically, it is not a drum (it doesn't have a drum head, for one thing). Its name comes from the steel oil drum it has been made of, the top being hammered to produce different pitches. Steel drums, originating from Trinidad and Tobego, are also known as steel pans.

Latin percussion

Some of the best-known Latin percussion instruments are congas, bongos, timbales, and cowbells (see page 180). These instruments are the driving force in a salsa band, but they're also used in jazz bands, rock bands, and related types of groups.

THE INSTRUMENTS

Latin percussionists also use an almost endless range of other instruments to spice up the music, as mentioned before. Many of these instruments are also available in kid's versions.

More percussion instruments
There are many more percussion instruments. Each culture seems to have its own assortment.

- Some of these instruments are easily accessible for beginning players, such as the African **djembe**, which is often used in drum circles. The traditional wooden djembe is frequently replaced by Western variations with a modern tuning system (using tension rods and lugs rather than ropes), a fiberglass shell and a plastic head.

A Western djembe.

- The djembe slightly resembles the Turkish **darbuka**, a vase drum with a metal shell.

- Brazilian drums, such as the large **surdo** and the high-pitched repinique, are used outside of samba bands as well.

- Many other types of drums are rarely used by beginners, such as the Latin-American **cajon** (the player sits on this multi-toned wooden box while playing it), the Indian **tabla** (two small drums that produce a multitude of pitches and tones), and Japanese drums, like the giant odaiko, a drum that may weigh close to five hundred pounds.

COMPUTERS AND TURNTABLES

It took some time before computers and turntables were considered musical instruments, but they can definitely be used as such.

CHAPTER 9

The computer
Thousands of songs these days are composed, arranged — and played, and recorded — with nothing but a digital keyboard instrument hooked up to a computer. Many kids and teens love to express themselves musically this way. The computer houses sampled sounds (see page 201) of every instrument you can think of, and the player triggers these sounds from a piano-type digital keyboard hooked up to the computer. These sounds can be recorded layer by layer using the computer's sequencing software: first the bass, then the drums, a piano part, strings, horns, a guitar solo; the possibilities are endless. The music can also be arranged and edited on the computer (assigning other voices to parts; changing the key of the song, altering the timing or the pitch of single notes, and so on). As an alternative, there is software that provides budding musicians with all kinds of loops, beats, and sounds, allowing them to create their own music even without a master keyboard or another 'traditional' instrument around.

And more
The computer can also be used to burn the music onto a CD, publish it on YouTube or other websites, to print the scores of all the individual parts of the composition, or to record acoustic instruments, of course. Given the right software, you can make a score as you would on paper, then assign voices to the notes and have the computer play the music, and so on. The possibilities are truly infinite. The required software ranges from effective freeware to expensive professional tools with numerous advanced features.

Turntables
Originally, the turntable was nothing more than a record player, but it has turned into a valid musical instrument over the years. DJs entertain the crowd by carefully choosing and mixing a sequence of songs (changing their tempo, creating new rhythms by playing two songs simultaneously, and so on). Some DJs or turntablists join a band, manipulating their records or CDs by hand while operating one or more faders to produce percussive sounds, riffs, and special effects (from echoes and flare scratches to loopings and hydroplanes). Records, commonly referred to as 'vinyl,' are also used to add rhythm or harmonies to the music.

10

Being Prepared

A dry throat, butterflies in your stomach, jitters and shakes, weak knees, trembling fingers, a throbbing heart... All familiar sensations experienced by most anyone who ever climbed a stage to perform, audition, or take a music exam (and those who claim that they have never experienced such symptoms are often said to be lying or dead!).

CHAPTER 10

Nervousness and performing go hand in hand. It's a sign that you're undergoing an adrenaline rush. Without it, performances may be less exciting for both the musicians and the audience. But stage fright can get so bad that it causes people to fail an audition or an exam, or mess up the performance. This chapter shares some ideas on reducing audition anxiety, stage fright, and exam nerves.

Books
Many books have been written on this subject, and there is a whole lot more to be said and taught about it. The tips on the following pages touch the mere basics, and as obvious as some of them may seem, they're often quite effective.

Adults and kids
Kids seem to suffer less from anxiety symptoms than most teens and adults. One of the best ways to prevent such feelings in the first place is to inspire them to begin performing in public at an early age, be it with a school band, playing or singing mini-recitals for the family every now and then — even if it's only briefly.

PREPARING YOURSELF

First, a look at what could, or should, be done beforehand. As older kids may very well read the following sections themselves (and as many of these tips apply to parents as well), the text often addresses the reader directly.

Practice, practice, practice
Musicians who are not fully prepared for a performance, an audition, or an exam have every reason to be nervous. Practicing efficiently, possibly under the guidance of a teacher who should of course be aware of the upcoming performance, is one way to abate anxiety. A tip: The closer the time of the main event comes, the more important it is to focus practice sessions on problem areas, rather than on playing pieces that you already know very well. As a rule of thumb, you need to be able to play or sing the tricky bits

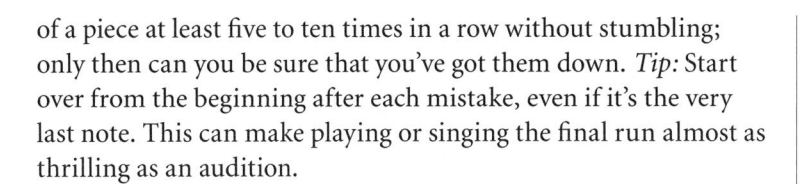

of a piece at least five to ten times in a row without stumbling; only then can you be sure that you've got them down. *Tip:* Start over from the beginning after each mistake, even if it's the very last note. This can make playing or singing the final run almost as thrilling as an audition.

Too late
Musicians who feel that they have to spend hours practicing the day before the performance, or on the actual day, have probably failed to use their previous practice sessions to the fullest. *Tip:* For horn players, practicing too long or too briefly in advance may cause them to have lip trouble during the performance.

Slips
Even professionals make mistakes, so preparing a piece includes preparing for stumbles and slips. Musicians should practice how to recover quickly and continue to play in the correct tempo. There are various ways to deal with slip-ups. Two tips:

- Do not **make a face** as this will just draw everyone's attention to the mistake.

- There are teachers who **specialize in audition preparation**!

Memory
You may play or sing from memory to impress the jury or the members of the band, but consider bringing your sheet music or your lyrics along if memorization was not required. Having it with you will make it easier to start over if you do slip. Does a piece

> ### Accompanist
> If you're going to play with an accompanist, it's best if that's the same person you've rehearsed with. Performing with a stranger can cause added tension, and a familiar face can be a great confidence booster. Even if not required, you may want to invite an accompanist. Having a befriended musician with you may help reduce stress, and it usually makes for a more entertaining performance too.

CHAPTER 10

require page turning? Then do memorize the first section on each following page. Another tip for auditions or exams: Make sure to make a list of the pieces you're going to perform, and don't forget to bring it with you. It really doesn't look good if you can't come up with the title of your next piece.

Deal with it
No matter how well-prepared you are, any type of performance will induce stress and nervousness. Dealing with this is part of the learning process of playing a musical instrument, period. Practice doesn't make perfect, but the more you perform (and the more exams or auditions you do), the better you will eventually become at handling stage fright.

Surrender
Trying to fight your nerves is not a good idea. It can even add to your stress level, which is probably already substantial. Telling yourself to be calm usually doesn't work either. You aren't calm, so it's actually better to just surrender to that. The fact that your nerves can make your performance less than brilliant just shows how important it is to be well-prepared.

Getting used to it
The more you're used to playing or singing for an audience, the less likely you are to be nervous for auditions and similar situations. Still, these situations are different from regular performances: They occur less frequently and there's usually a lot riding on them. A mistake made during a performance typically has fewer consequences than a slip at an audition.

Mock auditions
Staging mock auditions (a.k.a. placebo auditions or dress rehearsals) often helps in getting used to the extra tension. They can take place at home, while performing for family and friends. Teachers may organize mock auditions too. *Tip:* Turn mock auditions into a complete performance, including a formal entrance into the room, presenting yourself, and so on. Also, ask your audience to evaluate your performance afterwards to ensure that they were attentive to every note you played. Scary? That's the idea.

Recording in advance
Recording the pieces that you have selected can be very effective.

- Firstly, a simple recording device can have the same effect as an attentive audience in that it can make you nervous enough to perhaps make the kind of mistakes you would in front of a real audience. Getting used to the presence of a recording device is quite similar to **getting used to an audience**, so that makes it effective training.

- Secondly, a recording allows you to listen and **evaluate your performance**, as it's very difficult to do that while you're playing or singing.

- When evaluating your recorded performance, **don't listen for mistakes** only. Pay close attention to timing, intonation, dynamics, and all other elements that make for a great performance, including tone. Evaluating the latter requires good recording and playback equipment. *Tip:* First warm up, and then try to play or sing your prepared pieces and scales right during the first take — just like in real life!

Presentation
Are you required or do you want to dress a certain way for the performance? Then decide beforehand what you're going to wear, how to wear your hair, etc. Don't wait until the day of the show to do this, but get your look together at least the day before.

> **Sleep**
> And don't forget: A good night's sleep, or a nap before an afternoon performance, often works wonders!

SHOW TIME

There are many ways to reduce stage fright on the final day as well. First of all, leave home early so there's no need to rush, and make

CHAPTER 10

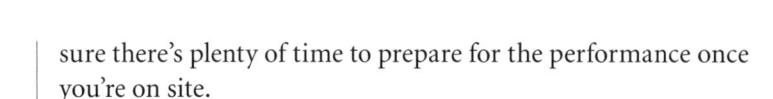

sure there's plenty of time to prepare for the performance once you're on site.

Relax

For some, simply repeating the words, 'I'm calm, I'm cool,' is enough to help them relax, but most people need more than this. There are many different techniques, ranging from deep-breathing exercises to meditation, yoga, or special methods like the Alexander Technique. You may also benefit from simple stretching, jumping, or other physical exercises.

Transfer your stress

Another idea is to find a physical release for your stress. For example, take a paperclip along and hold it when you feel nervous, imagining that all of your superfluous energy is being drawn into the paperclip. Throwing the paperclip away before you go onstage rids you from your stress.

> **Warming-up**
>
> *Warm-up routines (long notes, scales, and so on) not only get you musically prepared to perform, they can also help you relax. Long, slow notes are more effective than up-tempo phrases, obviously. If you feel the need to go through your scales and prepared pieces once more, you probably aren't really ready. Tip: Find a quiet place to prepare, if possible.*

Silence

If there's no opportunity to actually play before you go onstage, just moving your fingers over the keys or the strings of your instrument may help. Wind instrument players can warm up their instrument by blowing warm air through it.

The instrument

Make sure the instrument is in good repair, and thoroughly check it before the performance. Exam judges know that a string can break or a reed can fail, but even so, such events do not promote a confident performance. Brasswind players: If you've warmed up to prepare for your performance, make sure to drain your horn before going onstage.

Tuning
Tuning the instrument under the observant eyes of your audience, the jurors, or the examiners may be nerve-wracking, so make sure you take care of this in advance, if possible.

Try it out
Pianists will usually play auditions or take exams on an unfamiliar instrument. Find out if it's possible to try out the instrument you'll be using in advance in order to get used to its feel and sound. The same goes for other musicians who must use house instruments.

Holiday
Many musicians fight their nerves by conjuring calming imagery. They imagine that they're performing at home or on their favorite stage rather than in front of a jury; or they focus on a recent holiday, or pretend they're on a deserted island. Others promise themselves that this is their very last performance ever, so they need to give it all — now or never.

Pep talk
Giving yourself a pep talk may help too. But rather than just telling yourself to be cool and calm, tell yourself that you wouldn't even be here if your teacher hadn't thought you were ready. You have definitely earned being on this stage!

Focus
Don't focus on the outcome of the audition or exam. Instead, concentrate on your music, as that's really what it's all about. Don't go on stage to show how impressive a musician you are, but to expose the beauty of the music to the audience. Final tip before going in: Smile when you enter the room. This makes you both look and feel better.

A different type of audience
Auditioners and examiners are a particular kind of audience: They're there to judge your performance, rather than just enjoy

CHAPTER 10

the music. Still, it's good to realize that they're there for you: They want you to play or sing the best you can and they want to make you feel at ease.

Any audience
It may help to calm you if you look at your examiners and auditioners the same way you'd look at a 'regular' audience: Tell yourself that they're all very kind people. They usually are, so this shouldn't be too hard. Make eye contact with your jurors just as you would any other audience, and smile. And just as you might focus on the people you know, or on the ones responding favorably to you in a regular performance, focus on the juror who smiles back at you.

Imagine
Another approach is to completely ignore the audience (imagine that you're performing at home, all by yourself). This might not work at an audition or an exam, however. A popular method is to image the audience (large or small, jurors or not) sitting in their underwear, feeling even more uncomfortable than you are onstage. Or think of the audience as non-musicians who will be impressed by every single note you sing or play, or as the ultimate experts who showed up just to be able to hear you play.

The first note
Take a couple of seconds before you start playing. Breathe. Get the tempo of the piece going in your head, or even sing the first few bars in your mind. Imagine yourself playing the song. Then it's time for the first note. Make it sound great, and enjoy your performance!

AND MORE

If none of the above works for you, try consulting one of the many books on the subject. Another option is to take a yoga or meditation course, for example, or consider a drama class. Music teachers may have additional tips, and it can't hurt to ask friends how they deal with the problem.

Food and drinks

Various types of food and drink are said to make anxiety worse (e.g., coffee, tea, and other products that contain caffeine, sugar, or salt), while others help to soothe your nerves. Bananas contain potassium, which helps you relax, and there are various types of calming herbal teas, for example. Alcohol may make you feel more relaxed, but it definitely inhibits motor skills, judgment, and clarity — so avoid drinking alcoholic beverages at all times.

Drugs

Many professional performers take beta blockers (heart medication, actually) to combat their performance anxiety. This type of drug is considered relatively safe, and it works a lot faster than a yoga course and most other relaxation techniques. But you should wonder if music is your thing if you need drugs to do it, even if it's only for high-stress situations, like an audition. Try instead to reduce, if not eliminate, stressors; only do things that make you feel good, and avoid those that induce anxiety. Music is supposed to be fun!

Glossary

This glossary contains brief definitions and descriptions of some of the lesser known terms used in this book. Most other terms are explained as they are introduced: Please consult the index on pages 234–238.

Acoustic instruments
Instruments that can be played without an amplifier. The vibrations that are generated by playing the instrument are either loud enough to be heard (e.g., wind instruments, drums), or they are enhanced by a component of the instrument (e.g., the sound box on a guitar or a violin, or the sound board of a piano). See also: *Digital instruments*, *Electronic instruments* and *Electric instruments*.

Band instruments
Instruments that are used in marching bands, concert bands, and so on. They're mainly woodwinds, brasswinds, and percussion instruments.

Bowed instruments
See: *String instruments, stringed instruments*.

Brasswinds
Trumpets, trombones, baritones, euphoniums, and similar instruments are referred to as brasswinds or brasswind instruments. Brasswinds are also known as lip-reed instruments: the air column in the instrument vibrates as a result of the vibrating or buzzing lips of the player. Not all brass instruments are brasswinds: The saxophone, though made of brass, is a woodwind.

Broken chords
Playing the notes of a chord one after the other, rather than simultaneously.

Digital instruments
See: *Electronic instruments*.

Double-reed instruments
See: *Reed instruments*.

Ear training
Learning to recognize notes, intervals, scales, chords, etc. by ear.

Electric instruments
Mostly string instruments without a sound box. Lacking that acoustic type of amplification, the vibrations of the strings are picked up by one or more pickups or transducers that convert the vibrations to electric signals which can be electronically amplified. See also: *Acoustic instruments* and *Electronic instruments*.

Electronic instruments
Instruments that have no vibrating parts (reeds, strings, heads, etc.) that generate sound. The signal of the instrument is produced (and amplified) electronically. Instruments with a digital sound source (see: *Sample*) are known as digital instruments (e.g., digital pianos) or electronic instruments (e.g. electronic drum sets).

Fractional sizes
Violins and other string instruments (violas, cellos, double basses, guitars) in smaller sizes, typically for children. For example, a 1⁄16 violin is about half as big as the 4⁄4 full-size instrument.

Fretted instruments
See: *String instruments, stringed instruments*.

Horn
A term used by many woodwind and

GLOSSARY

brasswind players to refer to their instrument, whether it is a French horn, a trumpet, or a saxophone.

Instrumentation
The combination of instruments in a musical group.

Keyboard instruments
All instruments with a keyboard, such as piano, organ, and home keyboard.

Orchestral instruments
Instruments used in orchestras, such as violins, violas, cellos, and woodwind instruments.

Orchestral strings
The string instruments of (symphony, chamber, etc.) orchestras: the violin, the viola, the cello, and the double bass.

Percussion instruments
A very large group of instruments typically struck or hit (with bare hands, sticks, mallets, or other types of beaters) to sound. This family also includes instruments played by shaking (maracas, shekeres) or rubbing (guiro), for example.

Plucked instruments
See: *String instruments, stringed instruments*.

Reed instruments
Wind instruments played when a single or a double reed vibrates via your air stream. Clarinets and saxophones are single–reed instruments; the bassoon and the oboe are double–reed instruments.

Sample
A sample is a digital recording. Most electronic instruments use a large number of samples. A digital piano with 88 keys, for example, has at least 88 samples: one for each key or pitch. Any additional sound (such as another type of piano sound, or an organ) requires 88 more samples.

Single–reed instruments
See: *Reed instruments*.

String instruments, stringed instruments
Terms often used to indicate orchestral string instruments (violin, viola, cello, double bass) only. These are also known as bowed instruments or strings. Another group of stringed instruments are referred to as fretted instruments, such as guitars, mandolins, and banjos, or plucked instruments (which then includes the harp as well).

Strings
1. The strings on a stringed instrument or a piano. 2. The orchestral string instruments. See: *String instruments, stringed instruments*.

Wind instruments
Instruments that sound when blown, such as trumpets, clarinets, and flutes. Two main subgroups are woodwinds and brasswinds. See: *Brasswinds* and *Woodwinds*.

Woodwinds
The main woodwind instruments are flutes and reed instruments (clarinets, saxophones, oboes, bassoons).

Tipcode List

The Tipcodes in this book offer easy access to short videos, sound files, and other additional information at www.tipbook.com. For your convenience, the Tipcodes in this Tipbook have been listed below.

Tipcode	Topic	Page	Chapter
KIDS-001	A tuning fork	87	4
KIDS-002	Scales, chords, and broken chords	97	4
KIDS-003	A scale on piano	161	7
KIDS-004	Four clarinet voices	164	7
KIDS-005	A violin and a viola	185	9
KIDS-006	Various styles of music on violin	185	9
KIDS-007	Various styles of music on cello	185	9
KIDS-008	The double bass	186	9
KIDS-009	Nylon-string and steel-string guitars	187	9
KIDS-010	Guitar effects	189	9
KIDS-011	Various bass guitar sounds	190	9
KIDS-012	Flute fantasy	193	9
KIDS-013	Piccolo fantasy	193	9
KIDS-014	Four clarinet voices	193	9
KIDS-015	Soprano saxophone	194	9
KIDS-016	Alto saxophone	194	9
KIDS-017	Tenor saxophone	194	9
KIDS-018	Baritone saxophone	194	9
KIDS-019	Oboe and bassoon	195	9
KIDS-020	Trumpet and flugelhorn	197	9
KIDS-021	The piano	200	9
KIDS-022	A five-piece drum set	205	9

Want to Know More?

There's much information available on all the subjects covered in this book. The following pages offer a selection of helpful books, websites, and organizations. These listings are not intended to be complete, and the information is current as of the publication date of this book.

BOOKS

There are numerous books with a wide variety of songs, musical games, and instrument activities for babies and young children. Your local book store is the best source for such publications. The following is a random list of books on music education, practicing, and related subjects.

- *Nurturing Your Child with Music: How Sound Awareness Creates Happy, Smart, and Confident Children*, John M. Ortiz (Beyond Words Publishing, 1999; 219 pages; ISBN 978–1582700212)

- *Music with the Brain in Mind*, Eric Jensen (Corwin Press, 2000; 110 pages; ISBN 978–1890460068)

- *Your Musical Child – Inspiring Kids to Play and Sing for Keeps*, Jessica Baron Turner, M.A. (String Letter Publishing, 2004; 240 pages; ISBN 978–1890490515)

- *Music Lessons: Guide Your Child to Play a Musical Instrument (and Enjoy It!)*, Stephanie Stein Crease (Chicago Review Press, 2006; 216 pages; ISBN 978–1556526046)

- *The Young Musician's Survival Guide – Tips from Teens & Pros*, Amy Nathan (Oxford University Press, 2008; 192 pages; ISBN 978–0195367393)

- *Growing Your Musician: A Practical Guide for Band and Orchestra Parents*, Tony Bancroft (Rowman & Littlefield Education, 2007; 162 pages; ISBN 978–1578866007)

Practicing

- *The Practicing Revolution: Getting Great Results from the Six Days Between Music Lessons*, Philip Johnston (PracticeSpot Press, 2002; 324 pages; ISBN 978–0958190503)

- *Not Until You've Done Your Practice*, Phillip Johnston and David Sutton (PracticeSpot Press, 2004; 120 pages; ISBN 978–0646402659)

- *The Music Student's Illustrated Guide to Practicing. An A–Z of everything students (and parents) need to know about the subject*, Philip Johnston, PracticeSpot Press, 2007; 376 pages; ISBN 978–0958190534)

WANT TO KNOW MORE?

- *Practice Was a Dirty Word; With Tips to Enjoy Your Music and Shine in Performance*, Ruth Bonetti (Words & Music, 2007; 96 pages; ISBN 978–0957886124)

- *Perfect Wrong Note – Learning to Trust Your Musical Self*, Westney William (Amadeus Press, 2006; 240 pages; ISBN 978–1574671452)

- *Music Practice Record and Assigment Book*, Gail Lew (Warner Bros. Publications, 2005; ISBN 978–0757921216)

WEBSITES
General information – US
The following websites offer lots of additional information and articles on a wide variety of subjects, as well as links to other websites:

- MENC (National Association for Music Education): www.menc.org

- American Music Conference – The Voice of Music Making: www.amc–music.com, www.amc–music.org

- ISME (International Society for Music Education): www.isme.org

- National Music Council: www.musiccouncil.org

- MTNA (Music Teacher National Association): www.mtna.org

- Music Education Online: www.childrensmusicworkshop.com

- Music Education Coalition: www.supportmusic.com

- The Children's Music Network: www.cmnonline.org

- M.U.S.I.C (Musicians United for Songs in the Classroom): www.learningfromlyrics.org

- NFMC (National Federation of Music Clubs): www.nfmc–music.org

- Parenting Central (The Suzuki Academy): www.parenting–baby.com

- National Band Association: www.nationalbandassociation.org

- IAJE (International Association for Jazz Education): www.apassion4jazz.net/iaje.html

General information – UK

- Pay the Piper: www.paythepiper.co.uk
- Your Child and Music: www.bbc.co.uk/music/parents

General information – Australia and New Zealand

- Music Council of Australia: www.mca.org.au
- Music. Play for Life (music advocacy program): www.mca.org.au/music.playforlife.htm
- Australian Music Association: www.australianmusic.asn.au
- Australian Children's Music Foundation: www.acmf.com.au
- ASME (Australian Society for Music Education): www.asme.edu.au
- MENZA (Music Education New Zealand Aotearoa): www.menza.org.nz

General music programs

- Music Together: www.musictogether.com
- Kindermusik: www.kindermusik.com
- Music for Young Children: www.myc.com
- Orff Schulwerk: www.aosa.org
- Kodaly Method: www.oake.org

Music advocacy

For information on music advocacy, visit:

- American Music Conference: www.amc–music.com, www.amc–music.org
- Music Education Online: www.childrensmusicworkshop.com
- Music Education Coalition: www.supportmusic.com

- National Endowment for the Arts (US): www.arts.endow.gov
- Save the Music Foundation: www.vh1savethemusic.com
- Music Council of Australia: www.mca.org.au

Disabled musicians
The following websites offer information for disabled musicians:
- E–bility.com, Arts and Disability: www.e–bility.com/links/arts.php
- Coalition for Disabled Musicians, Inc: www.disabled–musicians.org
- Disabled Drummers Association: www.disableddrummers.org
- Handidrummed.com: www.handidrummed.com
- Drake Music Project: www.drakemusicproject.org
- Music and the Deaf: www.matd.org.uk

Examination boards
- ABRSM (Associated Board of the Royal Schools of Music): www.abrsm.org
- Royal American Conservatory Examinations: www.royalamericanconservatory.org
- NYSSMA (New York State School Music Association): www.nyssma.org
- RCM (Royal Conservatory of Music): www.rcmusic.ca
- Conservatory Canada: www.conservatorycanada.ca
- Trinity–Guildhall: www.trinitycollege.co.uk
- AMEB (Australian Music Examinations Board): www.ameb.edu.au
- ANZCA (Australian and New Zealand Cultural Arts Limited): www.anzca.com.au

Finding teachers and music schools
If you want to find a teacher online, try searching for "[name of

the instrument] teacher" and the name of area or city where you live, or visit one of the following websites:

- The National Guild for Community Arts Education: www.nationalguild.org
- Music Teachers National Association: www.mtna.org
- Directory of Nationally Certified Teachers of Music: members.mtna.org/mtnareports/Teacher_Lookup.asp
- American String Teachers Association: www.astaweb.com
- VoiceTeachers.com: www.voiceteachers.com
- National Association of Teachers of Singing: www.nats.org
- PrivateLessons.com: www.privatelessons.com
- MusicStaff.com: www.musicstaff.com
- The Music Teachers List: www.teachlist.com

Music teachers – UK

- Music Lessons Now: www.musiclessonsonline.co.uk
- Musicians Friend: www.musiciansfriend.co.uk
- National Association of Music Educators: www.name.org.uk
- Incorporated Society of Musicians: www.ism.org

Music teachers – Australia and New Zealand

- Australian Music Teachers Register: www.amtr.com.au
- Australian Directory of Music and Speech Teachers: www.musicteachers.com.au
- Western Australia Music Teacher Association (MTA): www.musicteacherswa.org.au
- Victorian MTA: www.vmta.org.au
- South Australian MTA: www.mtasa.com.au
- Tasmanian MTA: www.tmta.com.au

WANT TO KNOW MORE?

- New South Wales MTA: www.musicnsw.com.au
- IRMT (Institute of Registered Music Teachers of New Zealand): www.irmt.org.nz

Miscellaneous

- Little Kids Rock (Provides free lessons and instruments in public elementary schools): www.littlekidsrock.org
- Guitars in the Classroom (Promotes guitar programs in schools): www.guitarsintheclassroom.org
- Caras Band Aid Program (Provides grants to Canadian schools): www.carasonline.ca
- Youth Music (Facilitates music making for children and teens): www.youthmusic.org.uk
- Children's Music Web: www.childrensmusic.org
- Kididdles: www.kididdles.com

Essential Data

Four pages for essential information on band directors, music teachers, instruments, and so on.

Childs name:

Music teacher:

Email: Phone:

Instrumental teacher:

Email: Phone:

Music school

Email: Phone:

Music store:

Email: Phone:

Childs name:

Band/orchestra director:

Email: Phone:

Music teacher:

Email: Phone:

Instrumental teacher:

Email: Phone:

Music school

Email: Phone:

Music store:

Email: Phone:

Childs name:

Band/orchestra director:

Email: Phone:

Music teacher:

Email: Phone:

Instrumental teacher:

Email: Phone:

Music school

Email: Phone:

Music store:

Email: Phone:

ESSENTIAL DATA

Childs name:

Band/orchestra director:

Email: Phone:

Music teacher:

Email: Phone:

Instrumental teacher:

Email: Phone:

Music school

Email: Phone:

Music store:

Email: Phone:

Childs name:

Band/orchestra director:

Email: Phone:

Music teacher:

Email: Phone:

Instrumental teacher:

Email: Phone:

Music school

Email: Phone:

Music store:

Email: Phone:

INFORMATIVE WEBSITES

Organization	URL
	www.
	www.
	www.
	www.
	www.
	www.
	www.
	www.
	www.
	www.
	www.
	www.
	www.

INSTRUMENT DATA

In the event of one of your children's instruments being stolen or lost, or if you want to sell it, it's useful to have the following data at hand.

INSTRUMENT 1

Make and model:

Serial number:

Color:

Date of purchase:

Price:

Purchased from:

Email: Phone:

INSTRUMENT 2

Make and model:

Serial number:

Color:

Date of purchase:

Price:

Purchased from:

Email: Phone:

INSTRUMENT 3

Make and model:

Serial number:

Color:

Date of purchase:

Price:

Purchased from:

Email: Phone:

INSTRUMENT 4

Make and model:

Serial number:

Color:

Date of purchase:

Price:

Purchased from:

Email: Phone:

ESSENTIAL DATA

REEDS, STRINGS, STICKS, ETC.

It can be helpful to list the reeds, strings, drum sticks, or other accessories that your child is currently using to make re-ordering much simpler.

Brand:

Type:

Other details:

Brand:

Type:

Other details:

Brand:

Type:

Other details:

Brand:

Type:

Other details:

Brand:

Type:

Other details:

Brand:

Type:

Other details:

NOTES:

Index

Please see the glossary on pages 220—221 for additional definitions of the terms used in this book.

A

Absolute pitch: *148*
Accordion: *159, 180, 203*
Acoustic guitar: *150, 158, 186–188*
ACT, American College Test: *34*
Action songs: *25*
Adult teeth: *14, 59–61*
Advocacy: *34, 226–227*
Affiliations: *50*
Alexander Technique: *214*
Alto saxophone: *154*
Aptitude tests: *146*
Armchair memorizing: *108*
Athletic band: *170–171*
Auditory learners: *18*
Awards: *115*

B

Background brass: *157, 163, 197*
Balalaika: *191*
Band instruments: *220*
Banjo: *180, 191*
Baritone saxophone: *194*
Baritone: *157, 198*
Bass drum: *204*
Bass guitar: *144, 150, 189*
Bassoon: *36, 61, 63, 123, 144, 147, 156, 194–195*
Big band: *178*
Bongos: *158, 180*
Borrowing instruments: *124*
Bowed (string) instruments: *184, 184*
BPM (Beats Per Minute): *103*
Braces: *14, 15, 59–60, 61–64*

Brass bands: *172*
Brasswinds: *63, 149, 156–157, 195–200*
Broken chords: *97*
Buy-back plans: *129, 130*

C

Celtic harp: *159*
Chamber ensemble: *174–175*
Chamber orchestra: *174*
Children's instruments: *126, 152–160*
Choirs: *32* (flute), *39, 65* (signing), *162, 175* (clarinet), *176*
Chord diagrams: *58–59*
Chord instruments: *74–75, 164*
Chromatic tuner: *86–87*
Clarinet: *16, 60, 61, 155, 193*
Community music schools: *29, 36, 40, 41, 42*
Competitions: *71–72*
Computer (instrument): *207–208*
Concert band: *170*
Congas: *177, 180*
Conservatory: *32, 50, 67*
Contract: *115*
Cornet: *60, 63, 156, 163, 172–173, 196–197*

D

Digital piano: *89, 92–93, 94, 134, 201–202*
Dixieland: *178*
DJ: *208*
Double bass: *152, 159–160, 185–186*
Double horn: *157*

INDEX

Double-jointed fingers: *150-151*
Double-reed instruments: *194-195*
Down-sized instruments: *126, 152-160*
Drum (and bugle) corps: *72, 172*
Drum set: *93-94, 179, 204-205*
Drums: *203-205*

E

E♭-clarinet: *155*
E♭-flute: *154*
Ear training: *29, 39, 49*
Early childhood music programs: *13, 28-29*
'Easy' instruments: *153, 161-162*
Electric cello: *190*
Electric guitar: *150, 158, 177, 186-188*
Electric violin: *190*
Electronic drum set: *93-94*
Electronic tuner: *86-87*
Embouchure: *153*
English horn: *195*
Euphonium: *198*
Examination boards: *67, 227*
Exams: *66-71*
Exploratory programs: *31*

F

Field drums: *172, 204*
Financial aid: *41, 139*
Fingering: *105, 153*
Flugelhorn: *156, 163, 196*
Flute: *60, 62-63, 151, 154, 192-193*
Folk guitar: *187*
Folk harp: *159*
Fractional sizes: *14, 125-127, 152-160*
French horn: *36, 63, 122, 123, 147, 157, 197*
Fretless bass guitar: *184, 189*
Frets: *58, 59, 184, 185, 190*

Fretted instruments: *184*
Full orchestra: *171*
Fusion: *178*

G

Gifted children: *66*
Glockenspiel: *206*
Graded music exams: *67-69*
Grants: *34*
Group lessons: *19, 37-39*
Guitar: *5, 18, 24, 58, 59, 150, 158, 186-188*

H

Harp: *159, 190*
Headphones: *89-90*
Hearing protection: *94-96*
Home keyboard: *19, 24, 57, 94, 151, 162, 202*
Home school music programs: *35-36*
Home studios (teaching): *40*
Hybrid piano: *202*

I

Independent lessons: *36-27*
Instrument prices: *120-123*

J

Jazz orchestra: *178*

K

Keyboard instruments: *14, 89, 163, 200-203*
Kindermusik: *29, 226*
Kodaly: *29, 226*

L

Learning styles: *17-44, 45-46, 100*
Leasing an instrument: *125-129*

235

Left-handed players: *150*
Lesson fees: *42, 43*
Lesson times: *41–43*
Lever harp: *159*

M
Mallet instruments: *206*
Mandolin: *191*
Marching band: *107, 170*
Marimba: *206*
Melodic percussion: *206*
Melody instruments: *74, 75, 164*
Memorizing music: *106–109*
Method-centered teachers: *48*
Metronome: *85–86*
Mock auditions: *212*
Mouth harp: *203*
Mozart effect: *4*
Music advocacy: *34, 226–227*
Music for Young Children: *29*
Music schools: *40*
Music stores, types of: *130–131*
Music Together: *29*

N
New piece, practicing: *103–105*
Noise, how to reduce –: *89–94*
Nylon-string guitar: *158, 186–187*

O
Oboe: *36, 61, 130, 144, 147, 155–156, 194–195*
Off days: *115*
Orchestra: *171*
Orchestral strings: *14, 31, 125, 184–186*
Orff Schulwerk: *29*
Organ: *161, 164, 200, 203*

P
Pedal harp: *159, 190*

Pep band: *171*
Percussion instruments: *180, 203–204, 206–207*
Perfect pitch: *148*
Permanent teeth: *14, 59–61*
Philharmonic orchestra: *174*
Physical features: *13, 148–152*
Physical learners: *18*
Piano: *144–145, 158–159, 200–201*
Piccolo: *154, 192*
Pit percussion: *172*
Pitch (relative –; absolute –); *147–148*
Pitch: *12, 23, 91,*
Pitched percussion instruments: *171*
Practice, how long should you –: *76–78*
Practicing a new piece: *103–105*
Practicing techniques: *102–103*
Practicing, structure: *100–101*
Practicing, when: *79–82*
Practicing, where: *83–88*
Practicing: *73–109*
Pre-birth: *11*
Private instruction, private lessons: *38–39*
Progress, lack of –: *22–23*
Pull-out lessons: *33–34*

R
Reading music: *4, 13, 57*
Recorder: *153, 191–192*
Recording lessons: *54*
Recording practice sessions: *82*
Recreational music making: *75*
Reed instruments: *193–195, 220*
Relative pitch: *147–148*
Renting an instrument: *125–130*
Rent-to-own: *127*
Rent-to-rent: *127*
Rewards: *69, 77, 80, 100, 114*

INDEX

S

Sample: *94, 201, 202, 203, 208*
SAT, Scholastic Assessment Test: *4, 34*
Saxhorn: *198*
Saxonett: *155*
Saxophone: *16, 154–155, 194*
Saz: *191*
School music programs: *31–34*
Scramble bands: *173*
Secondhand instruments: *132–135*
Shadow practicing: *108*
Shakers: *204*
Show band: *171*
Sight-reading: *65, 68, 98*
Singing (for your children): *7, 11, 12, 13–14, 24–25*
Singing: *43, 162, 176*
Single horn: *157*
Single-note instruments: *74*
Single-reed instruments: *194*
Snare drum: *204*
Soprano brasswinds: *197*
Sound level, reducing the –: *89–94*
Special needs, children with –: *50, 64–66*
Stand band: *171*
Steel-string guitar: *158, 186–187*
String bass: *90, 185*
String instruments: *31, 184–191*
Stringed instruments: *184*
Strings: *184*
Strolling strings: *172*
Student-centered teachers: *48*
Studio policy: *51, 53*
Summer sessions: *55*
Suzuki method: *30*
Switching instruments: *16, 63, 128, 145*
Symphonic band: *170*

Symphonic winds: *170*
Symphony orchestra: *173–174*
Synthesizer: *88, 203*

T

Tablature: *59*
Talents and abilities: *147–148*
Teacher qualifications: *50*
Teacher, assessing a –: *49–52*
Teacher, learning without a –: *56–59*
Teacher, seeking a –: *43–44, 227, 228*
Teeth: *14–15, 59–64*
Tenor drums: *204*
Tenor horn: *198*
Tenor saxophone: *154*
Tenor trombone: *157*
Timbales: *180, 206*
Timp toms: *204*
Timpani: *203, 206*
Toms: *204*
Toy instruments: *12, 13, 26, 159*
Treble brass: *197*
Trombone: *149, 157, 196*
Trumpet: *149, 156, 195, 196*
Tuba: *157, 197–198*
Tuner: *86–87*
Tuning: *86–87, 96, 134–135*
Turntable: *177, 208*

U

Ukulele: *158*
Upright bass: *185–186*
Used instruments (secondhand): *132–135*

V

Varsity band: *171*
Vibraphone: *206*
Viola: *185*

237

Visual learners: *17–18*
Vocal groups: *176*

W
Wind band: *31, 170*
Wind ensemble: *170*
Wind instruments: *14, 55, 59–64, 149–150, 152–157, 191–195, 195–200*

Wind orchestra, wind symphony: *170*
Woodwind instruments: *195–200*

X
Xylophone: *206*

Y
Yoga: *214, 216*

THE TIPBOOK SERIES

Interactive Books with TIPCODES

The Tipbook Series

Did you like this Tipbook? There are also Tipbooks for your fellow band or orchestra members! The Tipbook Series features various books on musical instruments, including the singing voice, in addition to Tipbook Music on Paper, Tipbook Amplifiers and Effects, and Tipbook Music for Kids and Teens – a Guide for Parents.

Every Tipbook is a highly accessible and easy-to-read compilation of the knowledge and expertise of numerous musicians, teachers, technicians, and other experts, written for musicians of all ages, at all levels, and in any style of music. Please check www.tipbook.com for up to date information on the Tipbook Series!

All Tipbooks come with Tipcodes that offer additional information, sound files and short movies at www.tipbook.com

Instrument Tipbooks

All instrument Tipbooks offer a wealth of highly accessible, yet well–founded information on one or more closely related instruments. The first chapters of each Tipbook explain the very basics of the instrument(s), explaining all the parts and what they do, describing what's involved in learning to play, and indicating typical instrument prices. The core chapters, addressing advanced players as well, turn you into an instant expert on the instrument. This knowledge allows you to make an informed purchase and get the most out of your instrument. Comprehensive chapters on maintenance, intonation, and tuning are also included, as well a brief section on the history, the family, and the production of the instrument.

Tipbook Acoustic Guitar — $14.95

Tipbook Acoustic Guitar explains all of the elements that allow you to recognize and judge a guitar's timbre, performance, and playability, focusing on both steel–string and nylon–string instruments. There are chapters covering the various types of strings and their characteristics, and there's plenty of helpful information on changing and cleaning strings, on tuning and maintenance, and even on the care of your fingernails.

TIPBOOK MUSIC FOR KIDS AND TEENS

Tipbook Amplifiers and Effects — $14.99

Whether you need a guitar amp, a sound system, a multi–effects unit for a bass guitar, or a keyboard amplifier, *Tipbook Amplifiers and Effects* helps you to make a good choice. Two chapters explain general features (controls, equalizers, speakers, MIDI, etc.) and figures (watts, ohms, impedance, etc.), and further chapters cover the specifics of guitar amps, bass amps, keyboard amps, acoustic amps, and sound systems. Effects and effect units are dealt with in detail, and there are also chapters on microphones and pickups, and cables and wireless systems.

Tipbook Cello — $14.95

Cellists can find everything they need to know about their instrument in *Tipbook Cello*. The book gives you tips on how to select an instrument and choose a bow, tells you all about the various types of strings and rosins, and gives you helpful tips on the maintenance and tuning of your instrument. Basic information on electric cellos is included as well!

Tipbook Clarinet — $14.99

Tipbook Clarinet sheds light on every element of this fascinating instrument. The knowledge presented in this guide makes trying out and selecting a clarinet much easier, and it turns you into an instant expert on offset and in–line trill keys, rounded or French–style keys, and all other aspects of the instrument. Special chapters are devoted to reeds (selecting, testing, and adjusting reeds), mouthpieces and ligatures, and maintenance.

Tipbook Electric Guitar and Bass Guitar — $14.95

Electric guitars and bass guitars come in many shapes and sizes. *Tipbook Electric Guitar and Bass Guitar* explains all of their features and characteristics, from neck profiles, frets, and types of wood to different types of pickups, tuning machines, and — of course — strings. Tuning and advanced do–it–yourself intonation techniques are included.

TIPBOOK MUSIC FOR KIDS AND TEENS

THE TIPBOOK SERIES

Interactive Books with TIPCODES

Tipbook Drums — $14.95

A drum is a drum is a drum? Not true — and *Tipbook Drums* tells you all the ins and outs of their differences, from the type of wood to the dimensions of the shell, the shape of the bearing edge, and the drum's hardware. Special chapters discuss selecting drum sticks, drum heads, and cymbals. Tuning and muffling, two techniques a drummer must master to make the instrument sound as good as it can, are covered in detail, providing step–by–step instructions.

Tipbook Flute and Piccolo — $14.99

Flute prices range from a few hundred to fifty thousand dollars and more. *Tipbook Flute and Piccolo* tells you how workmanship, materials, and other elements make for different instruments with vastly different prices, and teaches you how to find the instrument that best suits your or your child's needs. Open–hole or closed–hole keys, a B–foot or a C–foot, split–E or donut, inline or offset G? You'll be able to answer all these questions — and more — after reading this guide.

Tipbook Keyboard and Digital Piano — $14.99

Buying a home keyboard or a digital piano may find you confronted with numerous unfamiliar terms. *Tipbook Keyboard and Digital Piano* explains all of them in a very easy–to–read fashion — from hammer action and non–weighted keys to MIDI, layers and splits, arpeggiators and sequencers, expression pedals and multi–switches, and more, including special chapters on how to judge the instrument's sound, accompaniment systems, and the various types of connections these instruments offer.

Tipbook Music for Kids and Teens – a Guide for Parents — $14.99

How do you inspire children to play music? How do you inspire them to practice? What can you do to help them select an instrument, to reduce stage fright, or to practice effectively? What can you do to make practice fun? How do you reduce sound levels and prevent hearing damage? These and many more questions are dealt with in *Tipbook Music for Kids and Teens – a Guide for Parents and Caregivers*. The book addresses all subjects related to the musical education of children from pre–birth to pre–adulthood.

Tipbook Music on Paper — $14.99

Tipbook Music on Paper – Basic Theory offers everything you need to read and understand the language of music. The book presumes no prior understanding of theory and begins with the basics, explaining standard notation, but moves on to advanced topics such as odd time signatures and transposing music in a fashion that makes things really easy to understand.

Tipbook Piano — $14.99

Choosing a piano becomes a lot easier with the knowledge provided in *Tipbook Piano*, which makes for a better understanding of this complex, expensive instrument without going into too much detail. How to judge and compare piano keyboards and pedals, the influence of the instrument's dimensions, different types of cabinets, how to judge an instrument's timbre, the difference between laminated and solid wood soundboards, accessories, hybrid and digital pianos, and why tuning and regulation are so important: Everything is covered in this handy guide.

Tipbook Saxophone — $14.95

At first glance, all alto saxophones look alike. And all tenor saxophones do too — yet they all play and sound different from each other. *Tipbook Saxophone* discusses the instrument in detail, explaining the key system and the use of additional keys, the different types of pads, corks, and springs, mouthpieces and how they influence timbre and playability, reeds (and how to select and adjust them) and much more. Fingering charts are also included!

THE TIPBOOK SERIES

Interactive Books with TIPCODES

Tipbook Trumpet and Trombone, Flugelhorn and Cornet — $14.99
The Tipbook on brass instruments focuses on the smaller horns listed in the title. It explains all of the jargon you come across when you're out to buy or rent an instrument, from bell material to the shape of the bore, the leadpipe, valves and valve slides, and all other elements of the horn. Mouthpieces, a crucial choice for the sound and playability of all brasswinds, are covered in a separate chapter.

Tipbook Violin and Viola — $14.95
Tipbook Violin and Viola covers a wide range of subjects, ranging from an explanation of different types of tuning pegs, fine tuners, and tailpieces, to how body dimensions and the bridge may influence the instrument's timbre. Tips on trying out instruments and bows are included. Special chapters are devoted to the characteristics of different types of strings, bows, and rosins, allowing you to get the most out of your instrument.

Tipbook Vocals – The Singing Voice — $14.95
Tipbook Vocals –The Singing Voice helps you realize the full potential of your singing voice. The book, written in close collaboration with classical and non–classical singers and teachers, allows you to discover the world's most personal and precious instrument without reminding you of anatomy class. Topics include breathing and breath support, singing loudly without hurting your voice, singing in tune, the timbre of your voice, articulation, registers and ranges, memorizing lyrics, and more. The main purpose of the chapter on voice care is to prevent problems.

International editions
The Tipbook Series is also available in Spanish, French, German, Dutch, Italian, and Chinese. For more information, please visit us at www.tipbook.com.

Interactive Books with TIPCODES

TIPBOOK MUSIC FOR KIDS AND TEENS

Tipbook Series Music and Musical Instruments

Tipbook Acoustic Guitar
ISBN 978-1-4234-4275-2, HL00332373 — $14.95

Tipbook Amplifiers and Effects
ISBN 978-1-4234-6277-4, HL00332776 — $14.99

Tipbook Cello
ISBN 978-1-4234-5623-0, HL00331904 — $14.95

Tipbook Clarinet
ISBN 978-1-4234-6524-9, HL00332803 — $14.99

Tipbook Drums
ISBN 978-90-8767-102-0, HL00331474 — $14.95

Tipbook Electric Guitar and Bass Guitar
ISBN 978-1-4234-4274-5, HL00332372 — $14.95

Tipbook Flute and Piccolo
ISBN 978-1-4234-6525-6, HL00332804 — $14.99

Tipbook Home Keyboard and Digital Piano
ISBN 978-1-4234-4277-6, HL00332375 — $14.99

Tipbook Music for Kids and Teens
ISBN 978-1-4234-6526-3, HL00332805 — $14.99

Tipbook Music on Paper – Basic Theory
ISBN 978-1-4234-6529-4, HL00332807 — $14.99

Tipbook Piano
ISBN 978-1-4234-6278-1, HL00332777 — $14.99

Tipbook Saxophone
ISBN 978-90-8767-101-3, HL00331475 — $14.95

Tipbook Trumpet and Trombone, Flugelhorn and Cornet
ISBN 978-1-4234-6527-0, HL00332806 — $14.99

Tipbook Violin and Viola
ISBN 978-1-4234-4276-9, HL00332374 — $14.95

Tipbook Vocals – The Singing Voice
ISBN 978-1-4234-5622-3, HL00331949 — $14.95

Check www.tipbook.com for additional information!